No Hiding in
The Open

A Journey in Professional Golf

John Hoskison
Former European PGA Tour

Also by John Hoskison

Inside - One Man's Experience of Prison
Name and Number
A Golf Swing You Can Trust
Lower Your Golf Scores
Your Short Game Silver Bullet

Author's note

Not long ago I was sorting through some discarded boxes in the loft, when I came across a file with 'Golf Story' written on it. Twenty years before, I had written about my experiences playing the European PGA Tour, but I had thought all records of the work had been lost.

When I read through the pages it took me back to a forgotten time, when I had travelled and played against some of the best players in the world. But they were memories from a different time in my life – maybe they should stay where they were.

Contemplating what to do, I sent the book to some friends of mine who had stuck with me through the good times, and the bad. It was they who suggested I publish it, along with the golf instructional books I had written.

This book is a record of my life on tour when I competed against the likes of Seve Ballesteros, Nick Faldo, Ian Woosnam and Sandy Lyle. It's a story about a young man struggling to find a solution to a problem; a golf swing that would withstand the stress of tour pressure, and not wanting to give up until an answer was found.

Reading through the pages I cringe at some of the things that happened, but the 'rock and roll' tour was very different then, to what it is now. We were a group of young men striving to succeed, but with little to rely on, other than our instincts. There were no psychologists, no one to ask for help in the dark days. We fought like a band of brothers in search of a common goal that eluded most of us, yet the journey was exhilarating. The following stories are about life on tour when we went into battle with blindfolds on.

Chapter One
Turning Pro

In good preparation for tour golf, I learned that life was not always easy during my first term at boarding school, when I was eleven years old. One of the sixth formers asked me into the senior common room. He stood in front of me with a pack of cards in his hand.

'Hoskison – do you want to play fifty two card pick up?'

It didn't sound too bad considering what was happening to the other new boys. I nodded. He went to the window, opened up the pack and threw out the cards. Unfortunately we were on the third floor and it was a windy day.

To avoid the habitual bullying, I became very good at sport; rugby, football, cricket, tennis. The academic kids took the brunt of the cruelty so I acted dumb and ran for my life. I became very fast over twenty-five yards – the distance from the senior common room to the bathroom, where there was a lock on the door.

After three years of hell, my parents took me back home and sent me to a day school, where they could keep an eye on me. They had been shocked at my dreadful exam results – last in just about everything. I must say, I didn't feel all that sorry for my former one eyed headmaster when he blew his head off with a shot gun a few years later. He didn't exactly run a tight ship.

It must have been a worrying time for my parents to have an academically challenged child on their hands. My father had gained a masters degree at Oxford University reading modern languages. My mother was a top professional pianist who had studied at the Royal Academy and my sister played violin for the BBC Symphony Orchestra. I was proving to be the exception to the rule.

However, in the safe confines of St John's Leatherhead, within a year of starting at the school, I had gained eight 'O' levels with top grades. I also continued to excel at sport and took up golf. I had never really considered golf as an option until one night I watched the US masters on television. Overnight, I became hooked. To support my passion my father started playing seriously and joined Effingham Golf Club where I became a junior member. He also fixed up for me to have a lesson from one of the most experienced teachers in Europe – John Jacobs.

Within two years I had won the Surrey Boys by eight shots, the Surrey Under 23's, as a sixteen year old, and in the summer of 1975 was picked for the England Boys Squad. After three years of freedom on the fairways, I wanted nothing more than to become a professional golfer.

When I sat my parents down and discussed the subject they were all for the idea, but they were keen for me to try a normal job first. Becoming a pro golfer was a big decision and they wanted me to get it right.

For six months I therefore worked in one of the largest banks in London, but I couldn't cope with the hassle of commuting, crammed into trains and buses and almost as soon as I started, I was serving out my notice. The world of banking proved no match for my Open Championship dream.

Once my mind was made up my parents, fully realizing the need for proper training, helped me find my first job in golf. Not wanting me to become stifled in the wrong environment, they hunted throughout the local area in search of a club with an older, experienced club professional, who would neither be jealous nor envious of an up and coming player.

Jack Busson was that professional. A Ryder Cup player in 1937, Jack was head pro at the RAC Country Club in Epsom, and after a meeting between himself and my father, he agreed to take me on. On January 1st 1976, when I turned up to sign my professional contract at the tender age of seventeen, no one could have been happier, nor full of expectation.

That first morning Jack (Mr Busson to me), took me to the practice ground to watch me hit balls. I literally threw myself at every shot to show my 5ft 7in, 9-stone frame could hit the ball powerfully, and when Jack summed me up as a Triumph Spitfire, as opposed to Jack Nicklaus the Rolls Royce of professional golf, I was ecstatic. It was a couple of years later that I learned the Spitfire had the reputation of being an unreliable car, and I often wondered whether Jack meant I was a speedy little thing, or that I looked capable of breaking down.

Unfortunately, I'll never find out because Jack died shortly after retiring at the end of 1977 and I was never able to ask him the question. However, my first year as an assistant professional was a fantastic experience. The RAC was situated in three hundred acres of the most beautiful grounds and among its luxurious facilities were two courses. Every morning, after cycling ten miles from Dorking to Epsom, I would collect my clubs, nip out onto one of the courses and play a few holes before the shop opened. When I finished work I would hit balls until the sun set.

After a few months under Jack's watchful eye, I entered my first event, which took place at Effingham Golf Club and to the absolute delight of my parents, I won the tournament. It was only a small competition, but a win is a win and I had chalked up my first success. My 71 beat a field of fifty young professionals and I earned a cheque of £50.

My scoring improved over the following months and many members at the RAC started to take an interest. I was often asked out for games and I even had a regular slot on Saturday mornings partnering the Captain of the club, the celebrated television sports commentator, Kenneth Wolstenholme.

The games became the highlight of my week. Many of our opponents were successful businessmen and one thing they all seemed to have in common was a fierce competitive instinct. Apart from having to perform for them as a golfer and help them with their games, I was fascinated to hear the stories they had to tell. Having had a rather sheltered upbringing at boarding school, hearing stories of corporate take-over's, which horse to run at Ascot and who to invite to the 'box' on Derby Day, I found immensely entertaining. We had some great battles that year, fortunately winning nearly every one. In fact the only thing that proved difficult was sneaking a cigarette on the course without the members noticing. Feeling they might not think it prudent for a young athlete to smoke, I devised a plan that enabled me to indulge my habit.

The fourth hole on the West course runs parallel to the boundary fence and a thick wood runs the full length from tee to green. My rather crude plan entailed a dramatic block off the tee, sending my ball deep into the trees on the right. Once in the trees I would magnanimously announce that I alone would look for the ball and would send on the other players. I never smoked much, maybe five cigarettes a day, but once out of sight I would light up and walk the length of the hole having a good puff, only to emerge on the green adequately 'fixed'.

Normally, I was a fairly accurate driver of the ball and I know this habitual inaccuracy used to baffle the Captain. As I was obviously unable to work out the reason for my disastrous blocks, he would offer a piece of advice each week to help cure the problem!

The year went well right through until Jack retired. It was a great shame that he did as I looked up to my boss and he'd taught me a great deal; not only to do with the swing. The frustration of not being able to hit the ball as I wished had led me to throw a club one day. After Jack witnessed the display I never threw a club again. He was a very kind, generous man, but he was also pretty tough and even today, if I'm in danger of losing my rag, I simply think back to the rollicking he gave me and it's normally enough to keep me in check.

After Jack left, Peter Butler, another ex Ryder Cup player became the club professional and I spent the early part of the year re-decorating the shop. It was a frustrating time as I was no longer employed by the shop, but by the club itself. Not having had a successful assistant for some time, the members had decided to pay me so I could concentrate on playing rather than shop duties. Having to spend endless hours painting and fitting out the shop, I found immensely boring but I threw myself into the heavy duty labour of knocking down walls and building stairs and used the experience as a way to help build up my small frame.

In early spring of 1978 though, my world took an unexpected shot in the arm, with the announcement that the Martini International was going to be held at the RAC in May. It was a full European Tour event and after pressure from the members, I was given a special sponsors invitation.

As the day crept nearer to my first event on the European Tour, I started to work so hard at my game, my hands all but disintegrated with blisters and sores, but nothing could deter me. The thought of teeing it up against some of the best players in Europe is what I had dreamed of.

Finally the week arrived. Spectator stands were constructed at the back of the eighteenth green, the tented village was erected and the club was transformed. Everything looked utterly spectacular, and what's more, I was part of it.

Whilst Thursday was to actually see me in action, I still had a few duties to perform and early on Monday morning, I was on my own in the shop waiting to serve any customers. I was sipping a cup of tea when the door opened and one of the hotel guests came in. He'd arrived the night before and when I saw him, I almost choked. There, standing in front of me, was my hero - Seve Ballesteros.

In his hand he held his clubs and seeing my attention was focused on him, he nodded at the clubs and in broken English asked; 'You grip please?' Only the day before Seve had finished runner up in French Open!

I took the clubs and looked at the wedge wondering if it was the club that had almost won him the Open Championship in 1976. I studied the grips, they were standard, and we had plenty of them. But how many rolls of tape would be needed to thicken the grips correctly?

My parents had urged me to study French and Spanish for 'A' level and always encouraged me to use my ability at languages whenever possible. My father had taken his degree in French at Oxford University, but even he would have been surprised I'd be speaking Spanish in the pros shop at the RAC.

'Cuantos layeros por las palos?' I asked Seve, hoping he would understand, but pointing to the roll of grip tape on the table.

Smiling, Seve held up four fingers. 'Quatro, por favor,' he said.

After assuring him they would be ready in an hour he left and I was able to get on with the job. Upstairs in the workshop, I cut the grips off with the care of a surgeon and completed the job without a hitch. An hour later Seve returned to find his polished, re-gripped set waiting for him. He picked up one of the clubs, waggled it to 'feel' the new grip and nodded his approval. Inwardly I breathed a sigh of relief. Seve was arguably the best player in the world. To re-grip his set badly would have been the ultimate sin for any young assistant.

Before he left he produced a wad of notes to pay for the clubs, but I decided Peter Butler could afford to pay and it felt great waving the bill. He picked up his clubs and was heading for the door when he paused and turned back to face me.

'You play this week?' he asked in stilted English.
'Yes,' I replied. 'Yo juego esta semana.'

He smiled, walked towards me and held out his hand.

'Your name?' he asked.

'John - John Hoskison,' I said shaking the hand that was offered.

'Well, good luck John, bueno suerte.'

As he turned to go I reciprocated. 'You too Seve.' I felt I could get away with Seve, rather than Mr Ballesteros (but only just).

I phoned my friend Steve Andrews immediately. It was the best thing that had ever happened to me, the very best thing.

Thursday finally arrived and I'd never felt so nervous. It seemed everyone had come to watch; my parents, relations, all my friends and an hour before I was due to tee off, I was sitting upstairs in the engineer's workshop having a sneaky cigarette to calm the nerves. Since alterations to the shop had been carried out, I'd been spending more and more time with Colin, the head engineer, and we enjoyed a mutual love of golf and music. My parents spent most of their time in Northampton at their school and I lived alone. Often I would stay the night with Colin and his wife who lived on the complex. My electric guitar was stationed at their house and there was nothing I enjoyed more than jamming with Colin to the blues of Jimi Hendrix. (Bleeding Heart – Albert Hall recording).

Colin and I had become very good friends and I accepted his offer to caddie for me in the Martini, even though he'd never caddied before. Experience wasn't featuring too prominently in our team. It was my first major event, in fact the first time I'd played in front of large crowds, and I was equally naive.

We were both pretty nervous sitting in his workshop waiting to go down to the tee, when Colin received a call from the clubhouse informing him that a leek had sprung in the kitchen and could he fix it 'pronto'. I didn't realise it was unusual to lose ones caddie quite so early and we agreed that he would take my bag, fix the leek, and then meet me half way down the fairway after I'd teed off. I went to the tee with one ball, my driver and a tee peg. Looking back it was the most extraordinarily unprofessional thing to do, however, I knew no different and went on my merry way. That day Colin was called back to the clubhouse three times and in total I got through four different caddies!

I played fairly well in the first two rounds and coming down the thirty-sixth hole, I had a chance to make the cut, an incredible achievement considering I didn't really know what was going on.

The eighteenth hole is a par five and after two shots my ball was lying some thirty yards short of the green in two. It was five o'clock, the stands were packed and I knew I had to make birdie.

I'd never hit a shot with so many people watching but my pitch seemed to be perfect. Nearer and nearer it ran to the hole until it hit the flag and disappeared from sight. A tremendous roar erupted from the stands, which were packed with partisan members, and as I walked the length of the green to pick my ball out of the hole, I couldn't help feel very proud of my achievement. My first cut!

In the third round I added a 71 to my halfway total of 147 and in the last round my playing partners were Ryder Cup players, Ken Brown and Eamonn Darcy. Hardly ever having played a four round tournament before, my long game started to crumble and only through a magnificent putting display was I able to shoot a 72 for a total of 290. Emotionally shattered and drained with the effort of holding my swing together, I walked off the last green and retired to the relative peace of the pros shop, to enjoy the cigarette I had longed for on the course.

A couple of hours later I watched the prize giving ceremony from the store-room in the pros shop, which offered a great view of scene below. Ken Wolstenholme, the Captain of the club, presented the trophy to Seve Ballesteros who had won at a canter on 18 under. When he stepped forward to receive the prize, I clapped as loud as anyone, but where proceedings should have finished, Ken continued speaking.

'Whilst that concludes the official prize giving, as Captain of the club I'd like to make a special presentation to our own, very popular young professional, John Hoskison.'

I couldn't believe it!

I rushed out, struggled through the thousands surrounding the eighteenth green and when I finally made it to my Captain, the noise of cheering was incredible. I received Ken's congratulations whilst a barrage of photos was taken, and then, to make my week, Seve stepped forward to shake my hand.

'Well-played. You play next week?'

I looked across to the tour director Ken Schofield who nodded and explained that as I had made the cut I was exempt for the following week, which happened to be the PGA Championships at Royal Birkdale, the flagship event of the European Tour. As I walked back to the pro shop in a daze, I was stopped in the car park by Kenneth Wolstenholme.

'Great performance John – well done!' He shook my hand again.

'We were glad to see you not hitting your

ball into the trees at the fourth for your customary cigarette,' he said smiling.

I couldn't help but laugh - so he'd always known.

Chapter Two
The First Scar

The day after my success in the Martini International, I travelled to the seaside town of Southport for the PGA Championships. Not having passed my driving test, I caught an early train from London and arrived in the delightful seaside town shortly after lunchtime.

Apart from the Open Championship, the PGA is the most important tournament in Europe and as well as television coverage and huge crowds, it attracts the strongest field of the year. As I struggled down the high street, under the weight of all my equipment, I walked beneath huge banners advertising the event and felt extremely proud that I was now part of the European Tour.

After asking about hotels and guesthouses in the Tourist Information Centre, I was pointed in the direction of a road running parallel to the high street, where apparently there was no shortage of accommodation. It wasn't far and before long I found myself entering a road full of small hotels advertising vacancies. I'd never booked a room in a hotel before; in fact I can't remember ever having travelled away on my own. Apart from a brief sortie into the world of banking, which my parents had asked me to try for six months, I'd thrown all my enthusiasm into golf and had little time for anything else.

I must have looked a sorry sight struggling with my luggage, but it didn't put off the landlady who opened the door of the first guesthouse I tried. She was a pretty lady, about forty I guessed and she was very kind. She showed me to a single room on the second floor and told me that if there was anything I needed, I just had to ask. Seeing my clubs she asked where I intended to play. When I explained that I was competing in the PGA itself, she looked suitably impressed. She said she used to play herself, but since her divorce and her son had moved to university, her hands had been full running the hotel 'Will you be wanting B & B, or, for a little extra, bed and breakfast and an evening meal?'

Being on a tight budget and not knowing anyone to eat with, I gladly accepted the latter.

'Good,' she said turning down the bed for me. 'Shall we say, eight o'clock?'

She left me alone to unpack and as quickly as possible I threw my clothes into a cupboard and unpacked my clubs. Although it was quite late, and I was tired from the journey, I couldn't wait to see the famous links where Jonny Miller had won the Open Championship only two years before. I slung my clubs across my back and headed out for the bus stop.

Southport has long been used to hosting major golf championships, and the whole town was geared up to looking after the needs of spectators and it didn't take me long before I found a bus to take me to the course. It was a great feeling when I registered at the Tour office and received the congratulations of the staff on my success the previous week. After filling in forms, informing the officials where I was staying, and paying my entrance fee of twenty five pounds, I wandered to the locker room where I had been told I'd find the starting sheet for a practice round. Half an hour later I was standing on the first tee.

Wow - what a tough drive! I stood looking down the narrow tee trying to work out to how avoid the out of bounds fence on the right, the bunker to the left and the thick rough running the length of the hole on both sides. I tried to visualize the shot I needed to hit, but looking down the impossibly narrow fairway, all I could think of was whether I'd brought enough balls with me.

Royal Birkdale is a classic championship course and an extremely hard test. The fade I'd cultivated, that had threaded me successfully down the fairways of short inland courses, became an uncontrollable slice on the windswept links and after nine holes, battling against the elements, I finally appreciated the maxim of my old boss, Jack Busson.

'You can't call yourself a golfer until you can control the ball in a left to right wind.'

On the first hole, in the stiff breeze, I'd hit two huge slices straight out of bounds. On several holes, where the wind was blowing left to right and against, my drives acted like fighter aircraft. They would take off relatively straight, but then peel away to attack the fairway at an angle of forty-five degrees before bouncing cross the hard fairways into the rough. The thick rough! I'd never encountered anything as tough.

The ninth hole brought me back to the clubhouse, and with only a couple of hours left before I had to return to my guest house, I decided to complete my round the next day and opted for a confidence boosting practice session. I needed to find out how to draw the ball.

I walked off the course, collected myself a bucket of balls and made my way to the far end of the massive practice ground where the wind was blowing from left to right. There were only a handful of players with just a few spectators watching and I found a secluded spot where I could work at my game in peace.

Over the next hour I tried everything I could think of to draw the ball but my slice remained. The only way I could get the ball to stay left, was to excessively roll my hands through impact that resulted in a snap hook. I was becoming more and more frustrated at seeing such a massive spread of wayward shots, when after a particularly ugly hook, I took a swipe at a ball without aiming at anything.

'Four!' I shouted at the top of my voice, as I saw it slice away on the wind, ominously heading straight towards a group of people walking towards me. With some agile footwork a man leapt out of the way as the ball bounced in front of him. I breathed a sigh of relief, but I could see a few spectators were now looking at me. Out of embarrassment I changed clubs and nonchalantly hit a couple of pitch shots up the range, keeping my head down.

As the group reached me, I looked up to apologise and it was then I saw the man I'd almost hit was Greg Norman. I felt like dropping to my knees in worship. Although the White Shark had not grown his full set of teeth on the world scene, he was already being idolised.

'Sorry about that,' I apologised, feeling like a naughty schoolboy.

'Hey - no problem,' came the strong Aussie accent. 'You playing this week?'

'Yes,' I said.

'Well good luck.'

I half expected him to add, 'You'll need it,' but he carried on and found a space to practice not far away. About fifteen minutes after watching Greg launch missiles into the distance, undeviating in their accuracy, I decided to call it a day.

That night, during dinner, my landlady (Susan as she'd asked me to call her) joined me and I told her about my experiences at the club and how I'd nearly hit Greg Norman. I must admit, laughing about it made me feel better and when I fell into bed exhausted, I was starting to feel more confident. Unfortunately, that confidence was short lived.

Over the next couple of days my slice got even worse and my hope for a successful first round lay in one direction; a day without wind. Unfortunately, that looked highly unlikely having heard the weather forecast and I woke early on Thursday, not to birds singing, but a rattling window. I leapt out of bed to look outside to see trees bending and dust swirling up the road in mini tornadoes.

Confidence is a result of believing things will turn out all right, nerves are born from the unpredictable, and later that day, as I made my way to the first tee I was extremely nervous. My teeing off time hadn't helped. Due to my success the previous week, I was due to play with the South African golfer John Fourie, in a pairing directly behind Greg Norman and worse, directly in front of Mark James and Severiano Ballesteros.

At eleven o'clock the huge crowds, eager to see their hero in the next match, pressed in so tightly round the first tee that I had to push my way through clutching my small carrying bag to my chest. I think they thought I was a caddie. Had I been more experienced, I would have realised that any one of the thousands of spectators would have been delighted to caddie for me, but catastrophically, I ventured out alone.

For me, it was an impossible test. Not only had the wind swung round so the opening hole was being played in left to right wind blowing into our faces, but the enthusiastic crowd, understandably keen to see every shot Seve played, were charging round oblivious to our pairing. Twice on the opening holes I was disturbed by people talking when I was about to putt, but rather than stop and walk away, which is what I should have done; I didn't want to appear pretentious and missed both putts without causing any fuss. I needed someone to help calm me down. It was as though my senses had been switched to high alert and I had become conscious of every movement and every noise. If I'd been a horse, I would have been run in blinkers, but as it was, I continued alone like a nervous twitchy colt.

The round quickly slipped into one of survival. I started off with four bogeys in the first five holes but things fell apart on the sixth tee. If anything the wind had picked up. It was the toughest hole on the course and because Norman in the group in front was waiting for the green to clear, before we had a chance to drive off the pair behind caught up. Looking like a golfing God, Seve Ballesteros walked onto the small tee.

I thought he might recognise me after the previous week, and when he took a pace towards me with his hand outstretched, I thought he had. Momentarily I reached forward to shake hands, but all he wanted to do was to look at my club, my graphite shafted driver with the extra whippy shaft, possibly the whippiest shaft ever seen on tour!

He waggled it back and forth, the head responding about half an hour later, and after assessing the weapon, he grunted and handed it back. I knew what he was thinking - that it was a club for little boys, not a tour professional - and suddenly I had the distinct feeling I shouldn't be there at all, that I didn't belong.

When it was my turn to hit, my swing was so fast I was relieved to feel any contact with the ball at all. Instinctively though I knew it was a lousy shot and as I held my finish position I saw my ball shooting off along the ground. A bloody top! My saving grace was that at least it was a straight top, but a top nonetheless. There were thousands watching and the lack of applause was eerily deafening. The crowd was just as stunned as me.

As I stuffed the driver back in my bag and got off the tee as quickly as possible, Seve spoke to me. 'Bad luck Ian,' he said. 'Bad luck 'Ian'? I wanted the ground to swallow me up. It was only years later that I learned the name John, sounds very much like Ian when spoken with a Spanish accent.

I don't remember much about the rest of the round, nor the following day when the nightmare continued, but my scores of 81, 83 bear testimony to my appearance and brought me back down to earth with a bloody great bump. I had travelled to Southport full of pride and expectation and I was going to return embarrassed and humiliated.

I hadn't the energy or courage to return home after my second round, even though there was a train I could catch, and when I got back to the guesthouse I sat dejected, inconsolable in my room. It was one hell of a way to celebrate my birthday! My dreams off success and wealth had been literally blown to bits.

My landlady tried to be sympathetic and suggested a nice birthday supper together would take my mind off it. But what could she do? What could anyone do?

It was, in fact, only a few hours later after an excellent supper that I found out exactly what Susan could do.

'Have you had enough? Or would you like a little bit extra?' she asked clearing away the plates.

My confidence had been severely dented that week, but due to the incredible kindness of my brilliant landlady, my confidence wasn't the only thing I lost that week.

Chapter 3
The Future Lay in My Hands

Whilst humiliated by my performance at Royal Birkdale, rather than return south immediately, I decided to stay and watch the end of the tournament to see how the best players negotiated such a tough test. I was glad I did. When Nick Faldo was crowned PGA Champion I breathed a sigh of relief, his victory having laid to rest a ghost that had haunted me.

My decision to become a professional golfer was not a difficult one, after all, what young man would turn down the chance of such a marvelous opportunity. However, it was a brave one considering I harbored a nagging doubt I would not be good enough. My negative vibes originated from witnessing the amazing capabilities of several players on the junior circuit. Even though I managed to earn a place in the England boy's squad, several of my contemporaries were so good I almost gave up before I started.

Sandy Lyle, Ken Brown, Ian Woosnam and Nick Faldo were all on the scene at the same time and dotted around the country there must now be a select band of senior golfers still suffering from post traumatic stress, shell shocked from their early exposure to these golfing prodigies. Being on the receiving end of world-class golf at the tender age of sixteen is a shock to the system and we probably needed counseling!

I played with Faldo for the first time at Moor Park in the Carris Boys Trophy. He was like a giant towering above me and from the quality of his first shot it was obvious he was something special. His irons for safety drilled past my best drives and throughout he played majestic golf.

My first Faldo drubbing depressed me enormously.

'Maybe he'll win the Open one day,' my father said in a daze. I could have handled the Faldo syndrome, simply an anomaly as Jonah Lomu was to the world of rugby, but shortly after I played with a little Welshman who turned up on the tee with socks for headcovers. Ian Woosnam proceeded to hit off with stunning power. On the first at Hoylake his ball was still climbing as it soared over my childish effort.

Then at sixteen I witnessed Sandy Lyle hit a one iron. It was snowing; no one else could reach the green. He stood up and hit this shot with such awesome power it left us giggling with delight. The chances of having three US Masters Champions in the junior ranks, at the same time, seemed highly improbable. Only the passage of time proved it was an exceptional era.

Shorty after I'd turned pro I was given the dubious opportunity of playing with Faldo again. I'd just finished a long practice session at the RAC and was wandering into the shop when Jack Busson called me over.

'We've just had someone on the phone who's recently turned pro - wants to come down for a round.'

'Who is it?' I asked.

'Faldo - Nick Faldo. Are you going to go out with him?'

On a drizzly morning a few days later Faldo

turned up with his caddie and the three of us set off. People forget how powerful he was. When Faldo reinvented his golf game in the mid eighties he sacrificed power for control, but as a young man operating at full throttle, his length was genuine world class.

After a two-year break I was subjected to another exhibition of his genius and as before it shocked and depressed me. He hit one shot I'll remember forever. On the fourth hole he drilled a three iron with such animalistic power the ball climbed, then rose again with second flight and hung in the air for an eternity, before dropping next to the pin. The divot was about a foot long, the strike so pure I can feel it to this day. Nick Faldo's victory in the 1978 PGA Championships finally converted his potential and proved he was that good. It also made me realise two champions in the form of Lyle and Woosnam were simply lying dormant.

Travelling south by train, less than twenty-four hours after watching the birth of a legend, I was already devising a plan to become a better player. My own performance, although dreadful, had not made me lose my ambition to achieve success; rather it had given me a direction in which to channel my enthusiasm. My overwhelming priority was to rid myself of my slice and develop a shot that would fly from right-to-left when I needed it. After watching the top performers at Royal Birkdale a draw seemed to be the magic weapon of the stars.

Jack Busson once likened the feeling of hitting a draw to spreading butter on a piece of bread, a fade was like scraping it off, and I was determined to spread the butter thickly.

Hitting hundreds of balls every day, I came up with a method of hitting the ball from right-to-left when I needed to. Looking back, it wasn't a natural draw, the result of coming into impact from the inside. It was more a case of aiming right, coming over the top and rolling my hands through impact.

Unfortunately, I didn't listen to the advice of my golfing friends who warned about the dangers of practicing one particular flight. My draw quickly became a semi controlled hook, knifing through the air with the topspin of a Borg forehand and my swing developed into a right-sided body lunge that made even Alex Higgins look stable. But to me, it was success. I'd changed the fundamental characteristics of my game, and when I occasionally snap hooked my ball out of bounds, it felt a lot better than slicing it out of play the other side.

Protected by calm conditions and the shorter length of inland courses, where I could use my natural fade, I even saw a modicum of success. Through July and August I played in a number of assistants events and found my scores were good enough to pick up a few cheques. As summer came to a close, time had kindly healed the traumas of Birkdale and once again I was the young player to watch.

During those months I lived a very isolated lifestyle. My parents owned a small house in Epsom where I lived alone throughout the week. Whilst I was totally addicted to my sport and spent every waking hour thinking about the game, I also longed for company and in particular a girlfriend. I might well have walked away from an all boys public school with eight 'O' levels, and been regarded as having potential by the members of the RAC, but at twenty years old, I was worried I was going to be left on the shelf.

Towards the end of summer it was with great relief that I met Ruth my first girlfriend, who was incredibly intelligent and who planned to study maths at Cambridge. Spurred on by her being at school in Hertford, where she was studying 'A' levels, I set about learning to drive. Eventually, I passed my test and in a roundabout way it was responsible for my first significant victory.

The day after the examiner gave me the 'green light', the local Alliance Championships took place over thirty-six holes at Walton Heath Golf Club. The tournament didn't clash with any tour events and consequently the field was particularly strong with a few well-known players using the day as a warm up. For me though, the tournament did clash with a significant event. It was the day Ruth's school broke up for a weekend exeat, and for the first time I was to drive through London, pick her up, and bring her back to Epsom for the night. I was passing into manhood.

For once, my normally rabid enthusiasm for golf was diluted by the prospect of the excitement to come and in a daze I nonchalantly thrashed my way through the heather of the Old Course to record a first round 71 and be joint leader. There were a lot of pros playing, some of vast experience, and even though my reputation was growing, 'Little Hoski' was not expected to hang on. Little did they know however, of my future plans and it was with gay abandon I snap hooked my way round the New Course in the afternoon to record another 71 to win the Championship.

People thought I'd handled myself really well 'under fire', but I'd other things on my mind and never felt the pressure. Perhaps the purists might not think it the most honorable of victories, but mind games are important in sport and diluting the pressure is a concept I've used to great effect in other walks of life since. The trophy was huge and as I drove up the North circular to Hertford, life was definitely looking rosy again. As much as anything, the victory persuaded me to enter the European Tour qualifying school that was to take place later in the year.

Being able to drive suddenly opened up a whole new life to me. No longer was I confined to the courses at the RAC and I started to visit local clubs. One day I drove to Cuddington Golf Club where a friend of mine was the assistant pro. Mike Henning was a bit younger than me and less experienced with regards to assessing players in action, and I was skeptical when he told me, the young tournament professional attached to his club was a good player. His name was Peter Hollington and he'd just returned from South Africa where instead of competing, he'd been laid up for three months having suffered a slipped disc caused by taking luggage off the airport carousel.

When I arrived Mike said Peter was out hitting balls and intrigued to study a possible adversary, I wandered to the practice ground to watch. It was a beautiful sunny day and I'd just emerged from the small copse of trees on the seventeenth, when I saw Peter in action for the first time. I was spellbound. After introducing myself I sat and watched, desperately trying to find flaws in his swing but witnessing the efficiency of a fantastic action. Shot after shot he ripped down the practice ground with his Lynx two iron, forming the neatest group of balls I'd seen. He was like a robot. I waited for the mis-strike, but it didn't come.

Over the next few weeks I spent every hour I could in Peter's company, trying to learn from someone who would inevitably make it big, but who was temporarily accessible. He was a complete golf fanatic. He could quote page and chapter from Hogan's book,

'The Modern Fundamentals'. His clubs had been worn out through practice and occasionally he would need to take a wood file to the calluses that had built up on his hands. After a full day at the club he would return home to the small flat he rented and before going out to work at a local restaurant, he would weight train in the confined space of his small lounge.

Apart from his incredible training regime, Peter lived like a monk. He would buy bone marrow from the local butchers and make soup that would last days. He lived and breathed golf and would let nothing get in the way of his twelve-hour stints beating balls. I felt incredibly proud that Peter would not only spend time with me but would also watch me hit balls.

'You'll never make it if you swing like that, it's crap,' was his first diagnosis. Peter never pulled a punch.

In early October I played with Peter in practice for the European Tour School at Foxhills Golf Club and remember the startling precision of his game. He drilled six two irons at the short eighth on the Chertsey course, not one deviating off line, and when I walked off the eighteenth hole, after two exhausting practice rounds, Peter went back to the eighteenth tee to play the last hole again. I was standing at the back of the green waiting for his second shot to come flying in when two pros I knew were discussing the best players in the field.

'This guy's the best player' I said, pointing at Peter in the distance. Considering I was so shy, I must have been incredibly confident they were about to see something special. The ball hit the flagstick from over two hundred yards.

If Peter had a weakness it was his short game, but I had no doubts he would address that department with the same fanaticism he'd shown when perfecting his long game. Two weeks later both of us won our players cards and was I thrilled at the prospect of travelling to tournaments with my 'guru'. But Peter had a flaw.

Two months later, after the first round of a local winter event I saw him in the locker room.

'I played with Jimmy Adams today,' he said. 'I'm going to have a lesson from him.'

'You're what!?' I said in disbelief. The last thing Peter needed was a lesson, even if it was from a player who'd nearly won the Open.

'You know he played with Hogan once. He said Ben manufactured shots much more than everyone thinks. I'm going to learn to shape shots more.'

Over the next couple of weeks Peter disappeared to Royal Mid Surrey, where Jimmy Adams taught, and during that time I didn't see much of him. The next time I did, I was shocked. His usual American style swing, a cross between Pate and Crenshaw, had become a narrow bent left arm flicking action. The penetrating, ball flight that was a characteristic of his game, was replaced by a weak flopping shot that would bounce and roll onto a green, not pitch and stop dead. It was catastrophe, but Peter wouldn't listen.

We fought and argued but I couldn't break him down. It's the most frustrating time I've had in golf. The problem was that Peter practiced exactly what he was told, but many teachers (Jimmy included) tend to exaggerate their instructions expecting their pupils to meet them half way. Jimmy hadn't realised he had a fanatic on his hands.

Looking back Peter should have known he was on the wrong track by the deterioration in his striking. But like the pig headed nut he is, he kept beating thousands of balls placing total faith in his tutor. I almost cried with frustration. I considered writing to Jimmy to point out he was destroying my friend and I should have done so. I've not witnessed such a destructive series of lessons.

Shortly before the European Tour got underway Peter pulled out of going abroad due to his awful loss of form. Not only did I lose my travelling companion, but also the person who I felt could sort out my swing. From that one experience, of seeing how the wrong input can be catastrophically destructive, I was never able to trust a teacher and without question that held back my progress. I'd only had one lesson in my life until then. It was from the well-known coach John Jacobs who told me that my slice was due to my head position at address. I'd tried the change for a day and dismissed it quickly as my slice turned into a block cut that got me into even more trouble. Years later I came to understand that John Jacob's advice was right and I simply hadn't given the change long enough to work. The decision not to stick with his advice cost me dearly, but they say you can't put an old head on young shoulders and I had decided to find the answer myself.

In the spring of 1979 I ventured alone to play the first five events on the European Tour; the Portuguese, Spanish, Madrid, Italian and French Opens. The trip turned out to be a complete disaster.

Chapter 4
Portugal and Spain

When I entered the departure lounge at Gatwick airport, for my first trip away 'on tour', I walked into an environment so foreign to me I immediately felt like a fish out of water. It was bad enough being the youngest and smallest out of the fifty travelling pros, but wearing a new blazer and sporting a neat short hair cut, only to find the tour 'uniform' was jeans, T-shirt and a days growth of beard, I might well have pinned a notice on my forehead announcing 'I'm the new boy and I know nothing'.

It didn't help when Randy Fox, our travel coordinator, introduced me to one of the three pros I was going to share a flat with for the duration of the Portuguese Open at Villamoura.

'John meet Rafe – Rafe Botts.'

I looked up at the black, six foot three inch figure towering above me and stuck out my hand in greeting;

'Hi Rafe, pleased to meet you.' I said enthusiastically.

'And you John,' he said in his West coast drawl. 'How ya doin?'

'Fine thanks,' I said. 'Have you travelled far?'

'Jeez yeah, started off from Palm Springs two

days ago. Probably stick around here for three or four weeks then head back to L.A. Life on tour eh?! You come far John?' I tried to make Twickenham sound exciting.

I'd only been abroad a couple of times in my life and only then by car to France with my parents. I'd never flown, never played golf in a foreign country, and I was only one of three pros from Surrey who had gained their tour cards. With Peter Hollington electing not to travel, I was very much on my own. It didn't help my confidence when Kenny, one of the Scottish pros I was going to share a villa with, went to the juke box in the departures lounge and put on Respectable by the Rolling Stones. It might not have been a deliberate dig at me, but being a middle class, well-spoken, ex-public schoolboy, who was dressed like a 'toff', it certainly felt like one.

As our Trident jet blasted down the runway and took off into a seemingly vertical climb, so my life's learning curve followed suit.

The first week I hardly saw anything of Rafe as he disappeared to spend time with some South African players. Kenny and the other pro in the flat went off to with the Scottish pros. For several days I hardly talked to anyone and played practice rounds on my own. But even though my initial impression of 'tour life' was different to how I had imagined it, nothing could blunt the excitement I felt the night before the first event. I remember sitting in a local restaurant, devouring a cheese omelette as I planned the tee shots I would be hitting the next day. Several hours later I wished I had stayed in. At three o'clock in the morning I woke up with the most excruciating pain in my stomach and I only just made it to the bathroom in time. For about two hours I threw up with a vengeance, all the time trying to keep my retching as quiet as possible so not to disturb my flat mates.   When the sun rose I knew I had to get help so I crawled out and knocked on Kenny's door.

'Christ, what's going on?' he mumbled, still obviously half asleep.

'Kenny I'm in real trouble - I can't move - help me.'

I hated troubling Kenny and felt very guilty when it was with obvious reluctance; he called Randy Fox, who in turn called the doctor. Eventually the doctor came, a good-looking woman who pushed and prodded my tender volatile stomach, diagnosed acute food poisoning and suggested I stay in bed. This was mostly done by sign language as she couldn't speak a word of English. She also wrote out a prescription for me.

'Supositorios,' she said handing me the note.

I tried my Spanish. 'Yo no comprendo.' I explained. She drew a diagram of exactly what I should do with the suppositories and left me alone to die.

Disregarding her suggestion to stay in bed, I managed to crawl my way round in 78, but when I tried to swing my stomach felt as though it had repeatedly taken blows from a Sandy Lyle one iron. The day after my stomach was even more delicate and I shot 84 to comfortably miss the cut.   My first event in Portugal was a bad experience and to his day, if I get so much as a whiff of Parmesan cheese, I break out into a cold sweat.

Next stop was the Spanish Open at the Torrequebrada Campo de Golf and I flew early to my hotel in Torremolinos where I spent the weekend recovering in bed. I was still weak when pre-qualifying took place on the Monday and catastrophically I missed. Although I was feeling slightly better, I had not been able to play a practice round and the sheer speed of the greens defeated me. I'd never come across 'grain' before and reading the putts baffled me. It was a disaster having to sit on the sidelines for the week and I was feeling very sorry for myself.

For the first few nights in Spain I had been on my own, but on Monday night my roommate for the week turned up. I was really surprised when Kenny came in and slung his luggage onto his bed. I decided he'd probably drawn the short straw.

'How's the wee mon then?' he asked. 'I thought you were dying back there.'

'Much better thanks.' I said. I was pleased Kenny hadn't refused to share with me and I was determined to get on well with him. I was starting to feel lonely and needed to make friends.

That night Kenny disappeared with his fellow countrymen but still not feeling up to a large meal, I stayed in and had a sandwich. We agreed however, that on Thursday, whether in congratulations or commiserations, depending if he had made the cut or not, we'd eat together. I needed to make friends and the atmosphere on tour was reminding me more and more of my old boarding school. I was determined not to go through that again.

But a week off – what was I to do? I certainly didn't want to waste time and I decided to go early to the course each day and watch how it should be done by the top players. And there was no one better to watch than Seve. On the first day I watched him hit every shot of the practice ground and then every shot on the course. Seve shot a disastrous 81 in the first round because he tried to take on an impossible shot on one hole and the risk failed. Although he had a rotten round, I was staggered how much commitment went into every shot. He hit hard and positively from the tee, and I realised I needed to swing with much more aggression. No longer was I going to guide and steer the ball round the course. If I wanted to be like a tour pro, I had to learn to commit to my shots and look as though I meant business. Suddenly I had a plan for the next event

Not only did I have a plan to focus on, I was also starting to feel fit and strong. On Friday morning I went down to the hotel golf net to smack a few balls away before catching the bus to the course for Seve's second round. I was just about to try out a few drivers when I heard a voice call out.

'Excuse me, excuse me?'

I looked round and in the far corner of the garden I saw a young woman on a sun bed waving at me. By this time I'd locked my mind onto my golf and rather it was reluctantly that I wandered across to find out what the problem was. '

'Hi – can I help?' I asked.

She looked up and propped herself onto one elbow, fully exposing her breasts.

'Could you possibly do me a favour?' she asked, at the same time as holding out a bottle of cream. 'Could you oil my back?'

I was stunned. I'd never been asked to do such a marvelous thing and I cursed my luck. 'Look I'm really sorry but I've got to go to a golf course in a minute I don't want to get oil on my hands,' I said holding up my club to confirm the explanation.

'Where are you going?'

'Down the road to Torrequebrada.'

'Where they're playing the Spanish Open?' she asked surprised.

'Yes,' I said. 'I'm actually a professional. I was meant to be playing, but I got food poisoning and didn't qualify. I'd love to help but I've got to work hard today. If you're around later...maybe then?'

With a last quick, but subtle, look at her naked flesh I went off to catch the bus.

Seve played fantastic golf in the second round but incredibly he missed the cut shooting 151. Golf is just like that sometimes – full of up's and down's and hidden surprises. No one could have hit the ball better than him that week, but he still missed. Even so, I had learned a great deal from watching him on the course and I couldn't wait to put the experience to good use the following week.

Later that afternoon I wandered down to the hotel garden to see if I could find Kenny to commiserate with him as he'd also missed the cut. Theoretically we were meant to be going out for a meal that night. I spotted him in the pool area and was pleased and disappointed at the same time. Lying on a sun bed next to him was the young woman I'd met earlier in the day. I could have walked across and chatted, but the old saying, 'three's a crowd' came to mind and I decided to leave them alone. I turned to leave but moments later I heard a voice call out that I thought I recognized.

'Hello there.' I looked round to see the girl enthusiastically waving at me and I decided to venture across.

'Feeling better then,' said Kenny. 'Saw you walking round with Seve.'

'Yes - much better thanks,' I said. 'How did you play?' I asked.

'Fucking crap.' There was a moment's silence.

'Come and sit down. Join us…Please?' said the girl.

I perched myself on an adjacent seat. I was no longer going out with Ruth, my fanaticism for golf had put paid to that relationship, and it was lovely to be in the company of a girl again.

'My name's Rowena' she said, giving me a lovely smile.

'John,' I said making sure I kept looking straight at her face and not letting my eyes slip down to her chest. The three of us chatted for a while and I learned that Rowena was on a trip around Europe. She'd been a pupil at the exclusive Beadales School and was taking a year off before going to Leeds University to study English Literature. Chatting by the pool was a nice way to spend the last part of the afternoon, but most of the time I was thinking about my golf and several times left to hit balls in the net. Eventually, the afternoon came to an end and Rowena started packing up her things. It was then I realized how much I was in need of her friendly company and very uncharacteristically I blurted out;

'Would you like to join us for a meal tonight?' I was genuinely staggered when she agreed and after arranging a time where to meet her, she sauntered off to the hotel. Immediately I felt embarrassed. It had taken me nearly two weeks to arrange an evening meal with Kenny and suddenly I had invited someone else.

'Hey Kenny I'm so sorry, I should have asked you first.' But he didn't seem to mind and we went back to the room to get ready for the evening.

At eight o'clock Kenny was still getting dressed and I went down on my own to meet Rowena. We sat together in the crowded bar and it was great having her all to myself for a few minutes. When Kenny arrived we walked along the sea front to a local restaurant where I ate my first full meal for a week. Rowena was great company. Purely by coincidence we'd both read Voltaire's Candide for 'A' level and I must say it's the only time I've enjoyed discussing existentialism! It was a great evening, thoroughly entertaining and I was ready to say goodnight after a leisurely walk back to the hotel but Rowena had other ideas.

'Let's go skinny dipping,' she said as we got near the pool. I didn't know what that was but I guessed when I saw Kenny ripping off his clothes. Moments later we were all splashing naked in the pool. We were swimming about, generally having fun, when all of a sudden Kenny threw out the question; 'Hey, Rowena, who do you want to sleep with tonight?'

I was so embarrassed. It definitely wasn't the sort of question my mother would have had me ask, but Rowena she didn't blanch and answered immediately.

'John,' she said.

There was a moment's pause, then Kenny swam to the nearest side and heaved himself out. I followed feeling awful for him.

'God, bad luck Kenny,' I said feeling the way one does when a playing partner misses a winning putt.

'No matter,' he said. 'Do the business now,' he said dressing quickly.

Looking back I can understand why her company was important to me. Nowadays on tour you have a 'buddy' system where players are shown the ropes by experienced pros. Teams of golfers travel together with nutritionists, physiotherapists, and psychologists to look after their every need. But I was alone and I can see why I so easily gravitated to someone who offered me friendship.

For over an hour I had the most marvelous time. Rowena was experienced – I wasn't. Afterwards, as we lay together, I should have been gloriously satisfied, but I couldn't help shake off the feeling guilty about Kenny and that I had probably well and truly blown any chance I had of getting on well with him. The prospect of travelling alone for the next few weeks was pretty daunting. It's easy to say I should have toughened up and not been so introspective, but at the time I was experiencing so many different things it was difficult to see anything clearly.

When the sun rose, I said goodbye to Rowena and left to get on the first bus to the course. She was disappointed and asked me to stay, but I felt I had to practice and left to try out my new committed swing.

On reflection I think this was the time I should have taken heed of Hogan's advice when he said, 'As you walk down the fairway of life you must smell the roses, for you only get one round to play.

Chapter 5
Madrid, Italy and France

Three days later I sat on the tour bus with thirty other players being driven to the Puerta De Hierro Campo de Golf, where we had to pre-qualify for the Madrid Open. There were about 18 places available from a field of 100 expectant pros. I had completely recovered from food poisoning and I felt strong and fit. Incredibly, we had single rooms that week in the Don Quixote Hotel so I didn't even have any awkward moments with Kenny and I was excited to be in action again.

From the results of the previous two weeks, my calculations showed I had a good chance of qualifying. But as the bus negotiated the heavy city traffic, some of the pros sitting in the seats in front started talking about the score they thought would be needed.

'There's better players here this week, forget what happened at Torrequebrada, you'll have to shoot one or two over maximum,' said one South African pro who looked about thirty. His baseball cap was tilted to one side of his head, he carried a pair of Classic leather Footjoy shoes that must have cost a bomb, and he smoked a cigarette with the butt torn off. He certainly looked as though he knew what he was talking about. It meant shooting 74 at worst.

The day before I had practiced on the course and thought it a pretty tough test. The greens were lightening quick and there were several doglegs that needed precise tee shots. I had thought that 76 might get in, but suddenly I had to revamp my tactics.

Five hours later I stood on the seventeenth tee two over par. I'd played pretty well, committing on most shots, but it was taking time to adjust to the greens. They were nothing like the greens back home and I had three putted three times. Two pars however would do the trick.

The seventeenth is a fairly short par three and I hit a good shot to the green, but the ball landed on the front and screwed back off the putting surface into a small depression. My chip shot came up five feet short and I missed the tricky left to right putt. In my mind that meant I had to birdie the last.

I hit beautiful drive right down the middle of the eighteenth and my second shot left me exactly eighty yards to the flag – a perfect yardage. It meant I could swing smoothly, knowing I had the right club in my hand. I hit the shot perfectly and the ball finished on line just ten feet short of the flag. I tried to stay calm as I walked to the green knowing I had to hole the putt to qualify. I spent ages lining it up all the time telling myself that I mustn't leave it short.

When I hit the putt instantly I knew I'd hit it too hard. I watched it catch the right lip and spin out some eighteen inches past. I was absolutely gutted. For a moment I stood rooted to the spot aware I had just missed qualifying. There's a moment when you miss a putt when you want to have it again. I suppose we get used to using the rewind button on a remote control. My brain was going at a hundred miles an hour. It meant another week off. I thought about my parents and what they would be thinking. What a failure I was turning out to be!

Moments later I regained my composure and walked up to tap in my final putt but full of disappointment, I didn't take my time and the ball lipped out again. I was more embarrassed than bothered by the extra blow - a miss is as good as a mile.

As I trudged up the steep slope at the back of the eighteenth green my legs felt like lead. But my dejection turned to anger an hour later as I watched the scores going up and realised that 75 was going to make it easily. If I had just two putted the last hole I would have qualified. If I'd tapped in the short putt, which I'd missed because I was unprofessional, I would be playing in the tournament. I wanted to go back and do it again. 'Can't I have another go?' my mind screamed. It was such a stupid mistake. If only I hadn't listened to the talk on the bus. But it was too late.

Back in the hotel I wanted to tell someone about my hard luck story, but as I sat in the hotel restaurant listening to the players, I realized that everyone had a bad luck story and I decided to keep my un-professionalism to myself. I was starting to be able to say hello to a few pros by this time and didn't want to come across as a moaner, so I shut up and suffered in silence. But I never forgot the lesson. The future is not set in stone – you just can't double guess it.

Looking back I hadn't really done anything wrong those few weeks. I was young and it was my first time travelling abroad with other players. I needed time to adjust to a completely new way of life. But I couldn't see that. I was beating myself up hard - too hard. I needed a 'time out' to reflect and rebuild; put things into perspective. Instead, almost on autopilot, I packed my bags and with the other unsuccessful players travelled on to Milan for the Italian Open.

****

You'd be hard pressed to find a more luxurious setting for a golf tournament, than the Monticello Golf Complex near Lake Como. The scenery was incredible, as mountains and lakes surrounded the course and for the first few days there wasn't a cloud in the sky. It was impossible not to be inspired. What made it even better was that I was to actually play in the tournament as I had qualified on the Monday and I couldn't wait for the first round to start. When I finished my practice round on Tuesday I was eager to copy out the notes I had just made, and wandered into the superbly stylish clubhouse to find a quiet table where I could concentrate.

The clubhouse was fairly full when I entered, but surprisingly a table near the window was vacant and moments later I was sitting in a comfy leather armchair overlooking the magnificent course. I ordered coffee and started to copy out the notes I had made, when someone started speaking to me.

'Excuse me,' said a woman.

I looked up to see an elegantly dressed lady standing to one side. 'Is this taken?' she asked pointing at the sofa.

'No, please,' I said half rising as she sat down. I smiled and returned to my notes. Moments later I paused to take a sip of coffee and could see the lady was trying to attract the attention of the waiter.

'Can I help?' I asked knowing it had taken me ages to order my own drink.

'No, it's all right, I'm sure he'll see in a moment.'

Sure enough, moments later the waiter arrived and the lady ordered three coffees.

'Are you playing this week?' she asked.

'Yes, I am actually,' I said proudly.

'Did you play last week in Madrid?'

'Yes I did, but not very well I'm afraid. It's my first trip aboard and I'm finding it hard getting used to everything.'

'It takes time,' she said. 'When Tony went to the States it took ages for him to feel at home.'

As if on cue one of the people she'd been waiting for turned up and sat down opposite me. My face must have been a picture, for sitting in front of me was the man who had inspired me to take up golf, my idol - Tony Jacklin.

'Morning,' he said nodding at me.

'Morning,' I replied searching my stunned brain for something interesting to say.

'Nice place isn't it,' he said, then nodded at my notes. 'Early round?'

'Yes. I thought I'd go out before the rush, it's a beautiful course.'

He smiled, lent back in the sofa and started to talk to his wife. Seconds later I felt a hand on the side of my armchair and I turned to see the other member of the group. Ben Crenshaw stood to one side, only bloody Ben Crenshaw!

'Your coffee Ben,' said Vivienne Jacklin. Ben nodded and smoothly slipped into the remaining chair. Everything Ben did seemed to be carried out with the same smoothness as his putting stroke. He literally glided into the seat and sat down in one smooth movement.

'Thanks Vivienne,' he said in his well-known

southern drawl. They chatted for awhile about hotels and flights and then Vivienne nodded in my direction.'

'This young man's on tour for the first time,' she said with a smile. 'Takes time getting used to things doesn't it Ben.'

'Sure does, as important as a good swing feeling at home,' he said to me, probably not realising that every syllable was irrevocably engraved into my memory. He pulled a packet of cigarettes from his pocket, took one out and then offered the packet to me. Incredibly, it was the first time an adult had ever offered me a cigarette and I accepted thinking that at least Ben and I had something in common.

After a short while they left announcing they were expected on the tee, but as Vivienne Jacklin passed, she paused and smiled. 'Good luck this week,' she said.

'Thank-you. You too, of course.'

Years later I played with Jacklin at Wentworth in the PGA Championships and one day, when he was commentating on television, he analysed my swing. I still have the tape. I'm sure he wouldn't remember the coffee he had with me in Italy, but I'll never forget it and importantly how it made me feel a little more comfortable. When Vivienne Jacklin tragically died a few years later, I felt terribly sad. Her few kind words were a great encouragement.

In the tournament I played with Jose Hunchak who had the most fearful temper. On the seventeenth hole in the first round, he hit a horrid shot and then, like King Authur hurling Excalibur, he threw his one iron into the middle of the lake. It may not be the 'done thing' but it was one hell of a throw. In the second round he proved it was no fluke by helicoptering his two iron in similar fashion. A dubious mantle, but in all my years playing tournaments I've never seen such a powerful display!

Unfortunately I missed the cut. But looking back it was hardly a surprise. Everything was so different from what I had ever experienced before and it was hardly surprising my confidence was taking a hammering.

In practice before the event I'd hit hundreds of balls and was feeling pretty good about my game, but on Wednesday, the day before the first round torrential rain soaked the course and when the tournament started, the fairways couldn't be cut. Without substantial core power the thick wet grass made playing long irons extremely difficult, particularly to the several raised greens on the long par fours. I needed a five wood but all I had were blade irons, and I found it impossible to dig the ball out with any real flight. My fourth week of failure and I started to long for home.

Winston Churchill once said that 'Success consists of moving from failure to failure without loss of enthusiasm.' But the last week in Paris I was all out of effort. A month away with disappointment at every corner had taken its toll, and my swing and brain needed a service.

The exposure to pressure during those weeks had finally cracked my golf swing and that last week on the tight Paris course, my snap hook came whipping back with a vengeance. When I missed the cut I can't say I was too disappointed. I yearned to return to England, my family and friends, and take stock of everything I'd learned. Retrospectively I realised there is a limit to the length of time an individual can continue making maximum effort with zero reward in return. I'd worked really hard during those weeks and without any success I was drained.

Years later, I was teaching golf to John Francome, the famous National Hunt jockey. I was talking to him about the similarity between horses and people. Our conversation turned to the first time a horse goes racing. He said that even if the horse has a chance of winning his first race, the jockey mustn't push it too hard in the final furlong. Above all else, the horse must enjoy the experience.

When I look back, I realise I was far too young and inexperienced to go away for a long trip without someone to travel with me to keep me confident. I learned a great deal during those five weeks but at what cost I'll never know.

Chapter 6
The Links Nightmare Continues

I can look back with fondness and even humor at my early tournament experiences, because I eventually managed to achieve some success. Had I never discovered a reliable golf swing, I would have condemned my early memories to the scrap heap as too embarrassing.

The problem was, I needed help to sort out my game, but after seeing how a teacher had destroyed my friend Peter Hollington, and dismissing the lesson John Jacobs had given me, I decided to try to sort out my own faults.

Nowadays, with help from 'guru's, sports psychologists and the video camera, the way to improve is relatively straightforward and very much a team effort. But in the late 1970's, sayings like, 'the harder you practice, the luckier you get', drove often clueless young golfers to practice endless hours, only to groove poor quality swings. Unfortunately, I was one of them. I would beat balls hour upon hour, hoping that sheer effort alone would be enough. It took me a long while to realise it's quality, not quantity that counts. It was a very frustrating time. I lived alone, practiced alone and often went for days oblivious to the outside world while forming plans.

Spending every daylight hour on the practice ground, I experimented with different 'feels', to try to find a swing that could withstand the severe test of the European Tour. I'd seen firsthand how well Faldo and Ballesteros hit the ball and I believed that the key to my success lay in improving my golf swing. This attitude frustrated my supporters. Good results in local events led many to believe only a lack of experience held me back, yet my analysis led me to another conclusion.

Yes, I was good enough to succeed locally, but that success simply exposed me to beatings when I moved up a league. As soon as I stepped onto the longer courses used by the tour, my accuracy deteriorated and my game fell apart. Deep down, I knew this had nothing to do with nerves and not being able to perform on the big occasion. This was due to a technical deficiency and after weeks of thought I came to understand the reason.

I was a small man and pound-for-pound, I was having to create more power for my frame than my bigger and stronger colleagues. In technical terms I had to commit to power at the very beginning of my downswing, whereas the stronger pros, with heaps of power, had time to make adjustments, a skill normally referred to as 'timing'. Unless I learned to swing the club perfectly, the fact I had to hit the ball so hard compared to my fellow competitors would always make me struggle.

This gave me three options from which to base my future strategy. I could try to make myself stronger, giving myself time to create 'smooth' power. Alternately, I could try to build myself such a perfect swing that, if I did 'step on the gas', accuracy was not lost.

Finally, I could confine myself to short but straight hitting and develop a pitch and putt game strong enough to birdie the par five's that my colleagues could reach in two. There was little I could do short term about my strength, although I started to train hard, so my new direction lay in trying to accept my lack of length and improve my short game. At the same time, I was determined to uncover the secrets of the swing that would allow me to hit the ball hard, without fear.

During the summer of 1979 I had become attached to Home Park Golf Club in Kingston, which was about five miles from the flat my parents had moved to in Twickenham. Ideally, I would have stayed at the RAC but living on a shoestring meant I couldn't afford to rent a flat and it wasn't practical to travel every day to Epsom.

Two huge practice grounds at the course, which lay in the grounds of Hampton Court Palace, gave me ideal opportunity to hit balls and it was there one morning, when hitting short pitch shots to the practice green that I met Alex Herd.

'Morning,' came a voice as I lobbed another high trajectory shot onto the putting surface. 'You should try running up a few if you don't mind me saying so.'

Well, I did mind. I'd been bombarded with advice from well meaning friends for several weeks and I'd had enough. But I was new at Home Park and it was out of politeness, more than curiosity, I turned round to find a small elderly man reminding me of how I'd look at sixty.

'Good morning,' I said. 'You certainly look like a man who knows what he's talking about.' The sarcasm went unnoticed.

'I'm not convinced about the lob that everyone's

playing these days,' he continued, undeterred. 'Chip shots are so effective.'

I decided to introduce myself - stop him in his tracks, 'My name's John Hoskison I'm the new tournament professional.'

'I know,' he said. He walked forward and shook my hand.

'My name's Alec Herd,' he said. 'My grandfather taught me the chip shot, always told me to get the ball onto the green as quickly as possible.'

'Did he?' I said now slightly peeved. Deciding to fully intimidate the man I suggested, 'Perhaps you'd like to show me?'

Without batting an eyelid he held out his hand, took my club and rolled four balls forward. Only two months before in Madrid, I'd witnessed a short game clinic by the master himself, Seve Ballesteros, and I thought it ironic I was now being subjected to a demonstration by an interfering old 'sage'.

I watched, surprised, as he struck the first shot perfectly, rolling the ball up the slope, straight towards the hole.

'Nice shot,' I said trying to keep the frustration out of my voice as the ball dropped into the cup. His second shot lipped out, the third and fourth stopped inches short. They were better attempts than mine and I had to smile.

'Your grandfather taught you well,' I said. 'Was he any good?'

'He won the Open Championship,' he said casually.

'Which Open?' I asked.

'There's only one Open Championship.'

'The British Open?' I said obviously misunderstanding.

'Sandy Herd, 1902.'

'Your grandfather won the Open?' I said incredulously.

'Absolutely. His brother Fred won the American Open, and my father was also a pro,' he said. Game, set, and match Alex Herd! I threw my head back and laughed.

'And I thought you were just a stupid old codger.'

Over the next few years Alex became one of my closest friends. Often he would accompany me to local events and our friendship and respect for each other was mutual. Without question he was one of the best wedge players I've seen, and if I'd been blessed with his touch, my problems would've been over - inherited ability, artistic, creative, stunning. If he'd been a thoroughbred horse, he'd have been worth millions. Ambition, or rather lack of it, was seemingly his only fault and he'd settled for engineering rather than golf.

That summer I had a fantastic time. My confidence returned and locally I won eight pro ams and two regional tournaments. It meant I had a few bob in the bank and as the season came to a close, I decided to venture north to Scotland to try to qualify for the European Open at Turnberry. Even though it was a links course, the same type as Royal Birkdale, it looked the sort of course I could play.

In 1977 I had seen Nicklaus and Watson, tear Turnberry apart in their famous 'Duel in the Sun'. It was one of the most exciting Open Championship' s of all time, both of them shooting in the mid sixties on the weekend. It certainly hadn't seemed too difficult on television and if I was going to be able to play any links course, this looked like my best option. With weeks to go I was feeling up to the challenge and couldn't wait for my next venture into championship golf.

To save costs I travelled to the West coast of Scotland with a local professional in his sponsored TR7. It was a nightmare journey. We had to stop regularly to blow up the back left tyre, which had a slow puncture and most of the time I sat gripping the door handle in fear. Phillip Loxley was a fast driver. When we got past Carlisle, we pulled into a service station where we hit an open manhole cover. It ripped the silencer off and we completed the journey sounding like a formula one car. My chauffeur thought it great fun, I was almost sick.

Before playing in the event itself I had to pre-qualify at Bellisle Golf Club, a local course not too far from Turnberry, but as far removed as you could get from the famous links in character. I was paired with an experienced Irishman, Hugh Jackson, and after thirteen holes it looked as though I was going to miss the mark by a couple of shots. However, I kept calm and with an incredible stint of putting, birdied the last five holes to shoot 69 and secure myself a place in the Championship. As always, my father was thrilled. Maybe this would be the event where my luck turned.

****

From the moment I turned up for practice I realized the course was vastly different from the one Nicklaus and Watson demolished in the 1977 Open. Gone was the wispy rough, it was jungle off the fairway, the wind was freezing, and everything was grey and desolate. It reminded me of the windswept countryside I'd seen on television, when watching programmes about the extreme training exercises of the SAS.

On Thursday morning, the wind was blowing so strong I hit a drive on the practice ground that pitched 180 yards. I had to wear two sweaters and waterproofs just to keep warm. It was impossible for me to swing properly weighed down with all the clothes – yet take them off and I froze. Very early on it was apparent I was going to struggle.

Sandy Lyle covered the first five holes in two under – that was an impossible feat! I remember watching him on the second hole looking like a warrior made out of steel, striding down the fairway seemingly oblivious to the wind; for the same holes I was four over. It was obvious there was a way to play the course though, because one of my playing partners led the tournament after the first round. Tony Charnley had shot a phenomenal 68. Tony Price, the other pro in the three ball shot 80. I struggled to a depressing 81. I'd found every thick piece of rough, every pot bunker and rather than being able to put to bed my experience at Birkdale, my links nightmare continued. It's incredible that you can play good golf for several months, and then have all your confidence torn away in one round. All I wanted was a quick return home to avoid further embarrassment and I arranged to meet Phil at the back of the eighteenth green the next day for the drive south. Fortunately, my group was out early, before most of the spectators turned up, and it looked as though I'd be able to escape with the minimum of pain.

When I arrived on the tee for my second round, all thoughts of a quiet inconspicuous round went out the window. At first I thought I had made a mistake with my teeing off time as so many people were gathered round the tee. Then I saw a giant leader board hoisted high on the shoulder of a particularly strong looking junior. I couldn't believe my eyes; Charnley -3, Price +9, Hoskison +10. The last thing I needed was a portable scoreboard, but next to it, there was something even more horrifying; a man with a TV camera.

I went up to the starter. 'What's going on?' I asked. His explanation made me panic. The cameras that had been booked to cover the tournament on television had been relocated to London to cover Lord Mountbatten's funeral. The BBC had decided that the one portable camera they had, would follow the leader. That was my playing partner Tony Charnley. Instead of a nice quiet round, I was going to be on Candid Camera.

By the time we reached the turn I had dropped six shots and had moved to sixteen over par. On the twelfth I hit a swinging draw that carried on the wind dwarfing my usual hooks. After taking one huge bounce on the adjacent airstrip, I was about as far left as you can get on any course. Going to find it was like going on safari. It was with kindness, I suppose, that a group of spectators followed me on my trek, but when one of them asked if I was a professional, I nodded with embarrassment. At least their fascination in my struggles was giving them good value for money.

Eventually I found my ball, but the rough was so thick I had to slash my way back to the fairway using up valuable blows. I was doing my best to contain my score but I was losing the battle to survive and after another three holes I arrived at an unprecedented score. I looked at the scoreboard to see what everyone else could see. Tony Charnley +2, Tony Price +12, Hoskison +1. Plus One?!

At first I couldn't understand why my score was incorrect, but then I realised what must have happened. The scorer must have run out of number two's! Only having two of each number, he could only post +1 for me, not +21. Only at Birkdale, had I felt so embarrassed about my score but at least luck was with me as the scoreboard hid the truth. Perhaps it would put a stop to the comments I was starting to hear when I stepped onto a tee. With only two holes to go, if we could all maintain our positions, I wouldn't have to walk down the last, in front of packed stands, with everyone knowing my true score.

At the seventeenth I needed to hole a tricky four-foot putt for par and was relieved when it slipped in the right edge. It now only needed Tony Price to hole his short putt for all of us to remain on the same scores. As Tony walked up to his putt, I wanted to tell him to take his time, to concentrate, the last thing I needed was for him to make a stupid mistake. But he didn't take his time - he rushed the putt. Fed up that he was going to miss the cut, he didn't take up a proper stance, and I saw the putt lip out from no longer than a foot. Tony slipped to +13 and as we headed for the eighteenth tee my score went up on the board; Hoskison +21.

I'll never forget coming down the last that day. For the first time in a tour event, a tanoy system had been introduced to inform the waiting galleries which pros were next on the green.

'And here comes match number four', said the commentator. He first said a little about Tony Charnley, he then a little about Tony Price. Then it was my turn. I braced myself wondering with dread what he was going to say. There was a long pause.

'And here comes Lionell Hodgkinson,' he said eventually. The lack of anything interesting to say, and the fact he got my name so wrong, graphically summed up my professional career.

At the back of the green Phil was waiting for me and after quickly signing my card I jumped into his car and still wearing my spikes, we headed south, back to the safety of my home.

Chapter 7
Many Happy 'No' Returns

When I returned from Scotland, I sat down and had a long think about my future. Various options presented themselves. Previous experience working in a bank meant I could go back into the city and get another job. Alternatively, I had three good 'A' levels and I could follow my friends to university.

However, after assessing all the avenues open to me, I realised that I was so passionate about golf; I wanted to persevere and try to improve. It wasn't about the money or the potential fame. It was about trying to solve a puzzle. Sure, I'd taken a few beatings, and I knew I would probably take some more. But I didn't have a girlfriend and I was responsible for no one. There was no point in getting to the end of my life, regretting that I hadn't given it my best shot. No matter how long it took, until I had investigated every possible theory, I would continue trying to find a swing I could trust.

In the winter of 1979 I took a job on the green staff at Home Park to earn some much-needed money. It was hard work but I didn't mind the early starts. My days were spent raking bunkers and cutting greens. At one point we constructed a new tee, using sledgehammers to smash up concrete slabs that we made into foundations. In the evenings I trained in a nearby gym, where I worked hard at getting stronger. Every spare hour I held a club in my hand and thought about my golf.

For years I'd virtually lived on the practice ground but had seen hardly any improvement. The solution seemed so simple - learn to swing the club well, but without the use of a video camera, and not able to trust a teacher, I didn't really know what to change.

What I did know was that on shorter courses I had success. In the early part of the 1980 season I won ten pro ams in the area and an important regional tournament that banked me £1500. I had decided not to enter any tour events and concentrated on earning some money for a change. But as the Jersey Open came round, time had eased the pain of Turnberry and I was lured into having another go at playing links golf. There were two reasons why I decided to have a go. First, qualifying took place in England only a few miles from my home. Second, a friend had offered to travel to the Channel Island with me.

Steve Andrews and I had started playing golf together as kids and he had offered to caddie for me in Jersey. That was great news in itself, but an old friend of his family was a member of the La Moye Golf Club, host of the Jersey Open and he had offered to put us up for the week.

Michael was a tax exile and lived in a huge mansion on the island. When Steve, a scratch amateur, had contacted him to ask if we could stay for the week, not only was he delighted, but as a member of the tournament committee he arranged for Steve to receive a sponsor's invitation to play. Although I was disappointed to lose my caddie, at last I was travelling away with someone and I was really looking forward to the trip.

In preparation for the battle in Jersey, I came up with a plan for the week. I would employ the same tactics that were proving to be successful in local events. I would tone down the power of my swing and make accuracy my priority. I'd won some good money in local events because of my ability to keep the ball in play. No matter what else happened, I would stick to my plan and hit fairways.

A week later Steve and I landed in Jersey, loaded our gear into a taxi and headed for the course where Michael had arranged to meet us for lunch. From his enthusiastic welcome he was obviously pleased to see us. I think putting up two competitors was definitely a feather in his cap. His exuberance was not even dented when one of his friends announced that he had Nick Faldo staying with him. It seemed Michael felt more comfortable with quantity rather than quality. After being introduced to numerous people we were eventually let onto the course.

Like most links courses La Moye's a tough track. Not because of its length or strategically placed bunkers, but more because of its location. The Jersey course is perched on top of a high cliff, fully exposed to the wind that blasts through the English Channel.

In practice my form was not bad. I chunked the ball gently down the fairways maintaining a quiet pace to my swing even when the wind was against. Sacrificing power for accuracy had limitations of course, and my strategy would inevitably place added pressure on my short game, but I'd lost control of the ball at Birkdale and Turnberry, and I was determined to keep my swing smooth from the top.

During my build up to the first round I managed

to stick to my plan and by the time Thursday arrived, I was feeling confident with my tactics. Steve was due off before me and we had arrived at the club earlier than I normally would do. It was during that time I made a mistake that ruined any chance I had in the tournament.

A long driving competition was taking place at the far end of the course and on Michael's suggestion we wandered across. From the grass mounds that surrounded the tee we watched as the giant David Russell bludgeoned three drives down the thin channel designated the landing zone. Bernard Langer then fired three bullets right down the middle. I knew what was coming and I should have been ready for it. There was no way Michael would let us walk away without me having a go. I should have had the confidence to say 'no', but when he made the inevitable suggestion and handed me his driver, I folded under pressure and before I knew it I was teeing up the first of my three drives.

It was a ridiculous situation. I was in Jersey trying to put into effect a plan with an emphasis on straight hitting, yet an hour before teeing off, I'd been sucked into a long hitting competition. Even with all the spectators watching I tried to stick to my straight hitting plan, but when an embarrassing silence greeted my first attempt I didn't possess the confidence to laugh it off.

I stepped up the power on my second drive, and although the ball landed outside the allotted area, I was pleased with the ripple of applause. On my third drive I really let go. Every muscle, every sinew went into creating speed. I caught the ball flush with a touch of topspin and the ball shot off knifing through the wind. Moments later the marker radioed in and unbelievably, incredibly it was the second longest of the day. With chest puffed out and feeling like a pocket Hercules, I headed for the first tee. Within minutes of arriving at the course, my carefully laid plans had been discarded and 'Long John' was going to bring the course to its knees.

I got away with my iron at the first hole, a par three down wind, but when I let go with my drive at the second Clive Bonner, my playing partner, gaped in horror as my ball left Jersey.

Over the next few holes I tried to revert to my former plan, but I was caught between the devil and the English Channel and my confusion introduced an astonishing unpredictability to my game.

Years later, an American professional named Danny Goodman likened suffering on the course to 'bleeding' (as in wounded). After nine holes I was in need of a transfusion. I went out in 42.

On my walk to the tenth tee, I was so embarrassed, I was tempted to slink round the front of the clubhouse and avoid looking at the huge scoreboard, but driven by morbid fascination I went to see exactly how my score was faring. I couldn't believe what greeted me.

Stevie boy, my closest friend, my very best buddy had saved the day. Out in 44, there was a player worse than me. He'd had a nightmare start; three, eleven, five! I had to smile at his score at the second - an eleven! Wow, even in a state of confusion I couldn't do that. I continued on my way, hardly confident, but a little more spurred on by the match Steve and I were now playing - head to head for last place.

I managed to make a solid par at the tenth but at the eleventh, a par five, I had a chance to make birdie. To reach the green in two I had to hit to my longest drive so I really poured on the power, but my technique just wasn't strong enough to contain the acceleration. As I came into impact, I could feel my shoulders spinning open. There was no compression at impact, just a massive glancing blow and from an ungainly finish position, I watched the ball slice away on the wind, burying itself deep in the bomb crater on the right of the hole. I looked at my partner, who was by this time getting used to me playing a provisional ball off the tee, and he simply nodded as I informed him my intention. Moments later I had another attempt, but this time made sure my shoulders weren't open at impact. My hands loved it. For once they were being asked to do something and they didn't hold back. This time the ball whipped off to the left in a huge hook. My third shot off the tee went relatively straight and stayed on the island.

As we had to spend time searching for two balls we let through the pair behind, but the green wasn't clear after our fruitless search and the group we had waved through suggested we continue. By this time I was utterly confused. I wanted to guard against another wayward shot (I was running out of balls), yet I needed to hit my ball with everything I'd got if I was to reach the green. I needed to give the ball height, yet the lie was tight. Disaster loomed as inevitably as Tiger Woods one day winning a major.

My downswing was a mixture of different concepts and I felt the head of my three wood crash down, jar into the ground behind the ball, and jump up at an almost vertical angle just clipping the top of the ball. It leapt up into the air as though startled like an antelope, and then dropped down only yards away. Out of the corner of my eye I saw Clive smile. When I glanced round the pair behind were grinning.

I couldn't blame them. I'd once seen Dale Hayes hit a trick shot just like it. As I walked to the ball I could feel my cheeks turning red through embarrassment. I was still trying hard and desperately tried to hit a good shot to show I wasn't a complete hacker, but incredibly the same thing happened. This time I could have caught the ball in my pocket.

Clive could no longer contain himself and the two pros behind collapsed in fits of giggles. Golf is a strange game and has the habit of kicking you in the teeth when you least expect it, so it's rare not to have players empathise when someone struggles. My trick shots however had been exceptional, but I couldn't laugh with them and I was too numb even to cry.

I finished the hole taking a twelve, the highest score I'd ever taken and my total soared to an unacceptable level. There was nothing left under the bonnet, no ammunition in the gun and I wanted to raise the white flag and capitulate. Unfortunately, I hadn't broken any rules and had no reason to disqualify myself so it was to Clive's sense of pity that I made my appeal;

'Clive, help me. I just can't go on. I'll mark your card but I'm going to say I played the wrong ball and disqualify myself.'

It must have been painful for him to watch my golf that day and with an expression that suggested, 'it's probably for the best', I was allowed release from the pain.

The next day, before our journey home, Steve and I were reading an article in the local newspaper about the first round. Steve had manfully struggled on to card '88', and should have been congratulated on his perseverance. If anyone should have taken stick it was me, but the article read; 'Many happy 'no' returns for Hoskison. On his twenty second birthday, John Hoskison unfortunately played the wrong ball and was disqualified from the event'.

I'd dodged a bullet but for Steve it was bad news. 'The only amateur in the field, Steven Andrews, shot 88 and finished the round in last place. His performance clearly demonstrates the vast difference between amateur and touring professional'.

'The bastards,' said Steve smiling at the injustice. Strangely enough, Michael our host didn't turn up to the club that afternoon to see us as Faldo shifted into top gear.

When I eventually escaped from Jersey and I was able to reflect on my performance, I was annoyed that I'd changed my game plan at the last moment. Maybe I could have scored better had I used the swing that was winning me money at home. It was like turning up for the Olympic Games having trained to run two hundred meters, then swapping to the marathon at the last minute. It wasn't the only reason I had played badly, but it was one of them. I made a pledge to myself that should I ever have another go, if I found something that worked, I would stick to it no matter what.

Chapter 8
Superstitions

Before I write this chapter, I have to point out that I was still only 22 years old, I had no girlfriend and I was a young fit guy. I was disillusioned and game to try anything that worked. It's not exactly a chapter I'm proud of but I think it goes a long way to explain that I was prepared to do anything to shoot good scores!

In the winter of 1980/81 I put on a stone in weight and twenty yards on my drives. I was even starting to shave regularly. I opened the season with a few excellent local performances and with confidence restored, I entered the Martini International at Wentworth where the galleries are traditionally massive.

In front of thousands I drove the ball well, putted solidly, made the cut and earned a cheque. The following week I travelled to Ganton for the PGA Championships, where I made another cut in front of two well known players, Mark McNulty and past Open Champion, Bob Charles. Two cuts on the trot – heady stuff! Unfortunately, I couldn't keep the momentum going as there was a break in the schedule but I returned home full of enthusiasm. The sniff of success had given me the incentive to work even harder at my game. I hit hundreds of ball during the day and virtually wore a hole in the carpet putting at home. There was no respite even when I went to bed. Every night I would wake up in the early hours, get out of bed and study my swing in the mirror. By the time I travelled to the Lawrence Batley in Leeds, I was wound up so tight there was no way I could play well.

Yorkie, the tour caddie who had worked for me at Ganton summed it up very succinctly after the second round. 'Yer fuckin' trying to hard – you've gotta learn to calm down,' he said.

Thinking about it, he was right. In the Lawrence Batley I felt fit to burst with the effort I was putting in. So, adopting a completely different approach, rather than return home I decided to go for a holiday before the next event in Manchester a week later. With clubs stuffed in the car, I drove to Harrogate just down the road for a few days R and R.

Harrogate was hometown of my old boss Jack Busson and for several years he'd been the pro at nearby Panal Golf Club. Even though I was taking a break, I still intended to do some practice and felt confident I would be allowed access to the course, being Jack's former assistant.

When I arrived in the small town, I booked myself into the cheapest hotel I could find, which doubled as the sleeping accommodation for the staff of the largest hotel in the area. It was a bit scruffy and in need of a paint job, but it was ideal as a bolt hole.

On the first evening, judging by the deserted dining room, it seemed I was the only guest staying there and during my meal I became involved in conversation with the waitress serving me. After telling her that I was taking a few days off and looking for relaxation, she asked me if I wanted to join the after hours staff party at a local club. It was a kind offer and not having to get up early the next day, I accepted. At ten o'clock I tagged onto the group and was thrilled to find that the only members of staff present were women. Since splitting up with Ruth I'd been devoid of female company and I relished the prospect of an evening in female company. The night proved to be great fun and for once, I didn't even think about my swing.

At about midnight I decided to call it a day and was pleased when Karen, the waitress who had invited me, said she would also be returning to the hotel. When we got back, I thanked her for a lovely evening, said good night and went up to my room. After about five minutes there was a knock on my door.

'Hello,' said Karen when I opened it. Karen came from Leeds, was very pretty and after watching a few frames of World Snooker on the television, she started to take her clothes off saying, 'I might as well stay the night.'

I don't know how film stars manage to sleep with the girl nestling up to them, but with Karen's head resting on my arm I didn't sleep a wink. I was also worried she might get into trouble as our rooms were out of bounds to staff, so I remained awake to make sure she woke in time so she could sneak out undetected. When the sun rose I was shattered.

After breakfast, even though I was tired, the sun was shining and I couldn't resist going to play golf that day. Lazily I wandered to Panal Golf Club on the outskirts of town and after checking that I could use the facilities, I found the course empty and rather than hitting balls on the practice ground, I went out for a nice relaxed round.

Normally bursting with energy, that day I was dog tired, my arms felt like lead, my eyes hurt, and in the hot sunshine I finished the round almost on my knees. When I counted up my score, I couldn't quite get my mind round the fact I'd struck the ball beautifully and shot 65!

That night Karen was absent from the dining room and it was one of the other waitresses who invited me to a local wine bar. It was my second invitation in two days and although tired, I found the compliment too much to resist.

The wine bar was a lovely little place, not too busy and over a bottle of wine we chatted until closing time. Karen's closest friend proved to be great company and I felt gloriously mellow in the smoky, candle lit atmosphere. It was unusual for me to be so laid back. Normally I couldn't sit still, but that night I was happy to let the mood take me and remain in one place all evening. When I got back to the hotel my whole body ached and I was ready to tumble into bed, but after being told the manager was not around, my date suggested coming up to my room for coffee. I agreed saying, 'You'll have to make it a quick one.'

After another glance at the snooker, which was proving to be somewhat of an aphrodisiac, the lovely Janet stayed all night. Even with her head resting on my arm I managed some sleep, but in the morning I felt like a zombie. After she'd slipped away, I tried to grab a couple of hours rest, but some form of primeval instinct kept sleep away during daylight hours and with nothing else to do, once again I headed for Panal Golf Club.

With my clubs on a trolley this time, I trekked round the course, but instead of playing the rubbish golf I expected, my weak body produced crisp iron shots, long drives, and a lovely touch on the greens. I shot another round in the mid sixties, and walked off the course more than slightly peeved. Surely practice and sacrifice were meant to be the key!

That night over dinner I received yet another invitation which I readily accepted. If nothing else I was determined to prove the secret of playing good golf was dedication on the practice ground.

Mary was a lovely girl and I felt slightly guilty when I invited her back to my room. Even though my eyes were bloodshot and I looked like a vampire, she agreed, and with a slightly trembling hand I led her to my chamber. I yearned for sleep, but I was now carrying out important research. The next day I was quite upset when I tenderly shot 66.

When the lovely Karen appeared in my room the following evening, I realised I'd been placed on a four-day rota, which I manfully accepted. I remained dumbfounded that at least on the course my technique continued to be superb. In total I stayed six nights, for five days I had shot in the sixties. When I packed my bags and waved good bye to three fantastic women, promising to return if I had the chance, I travelled to Manchester never having felt so tired, or perplexed.

Experimentation had always played a key roll in trying to improve my golf and there were few things I wouldn't try, but the new theory was a strange one, certainly not one I felt I could easily discuss with my father or caddie. But 'proof is in the pudding' and after carefully weighing up the prospects of possibly 'blowing' a tournament, I decided to air my revolutionary technique under competitive conditions.

Staying up much later than I normally would do, I was tired all week in Manchester. It was like suffering from jet lag, but I played well, made the cut and earned a cheque. It wasn't quite the same as having a lady to entertain me, but Yorkie told me I looked much more relaxed, 'like a real pro,' and my father, who came up to watch the last round was thrilled by my form.

'Whatever you did last week, do it again,' he advised.

The precedent had now been set and I was determined to keep the routine going during my next outing in the Jersey Open. After I arrived on the island and had completed my practice round at La Moye, and grabbed something to eat in my hotel, I headed straight for down town St Helier. This time I was determined to get things right. The nightclub I had a ticket for, kindly supplied by the tournament organisers, and was packed with golfers when I arrived, but it wasn't long before I met my trainer of the week. Janine was a nurse who worked in an old peoples' home near St Brelade's Bay and she referred to me as her 'part timer'. She was great fun, thought it hilarious when I told her my theory and proved to be an exceptional motivator when it came to training time.

I saw her every night and as the tournament progressed my body felt as if it belonged to someone else. Even with legs left strong from running, I could only stagger round the course. My eyes ached and at every opportunity I closed my eyelids to give them some relief. My hands felt bloated and even though summer, I felt cold. Every thing I was doing was contrary to what I had based my life on and the way I played made me feel sick. My shots flew off the middle of the club, boring through the wind as never before and it became obvious I had found the method of keeping my right arm under control. Tire out the body so it can't move and the hands have to release!

Although it was a full tour event, the tournament was played in a celebrity pro am format and in the last round I played with the comedian, Peter Cook. As we stood on the tee I was concerned about his health, he looked ghastly. I was about to ask him if he was okay, when he asked me if I was all right as I looked tired and pale! But another cut, another cheque and I started to worry I had found the secret. It upset me. Why couldn't I be like other players and improve with practice - golf practice?

The next event was the Coral Classic at Royal Porthcawl golf club in Wales. Like most sportsman I was superstitious. When on a winning streak it was imperative that I go through the same ritual and my priority, more than practice, was to find my pre-match partner.

At first I was worried about finding anyone as Porthcawl seemed to be a sleepy seaside town without much action, but there were two girls working behind the bar at the hotel and I decided to ask them out. Both were French and couldn't speak much English, which gave me a distinct advantage over the other pros staying there as I'd taken French A level and was pretty good at speaking the language.

One of the girls was quite short, but the other was really tall. The little one would have been perfect for me, but I quickly learned she had a boyfriend. Monique however, was keen to go out for a meal the next evening. We arranged to meet the following night and during the day I found out there was a Chinese restaurant at the far end of town that was not likely to be the host of any golfers. I was conscious that Monique was about six inches taller than me and to avoid any ribbing from my fellow pros, even though she looked great company, I thought it best to woo my lady in private. When I stood beside her I felt like a ten-year-old child!

The next evening, I met Monique in town and after a long walk we eventually reached the restaurant. I peered through the window and inwardly sighed with relief when there was no sign of any golfers. Monique, I found out, was six foot two – I was five seven. Looking back she must have had great courage to be seen with me!

We entered hand in hand and found ourselves a nice table hidden away at the back of the premises. After a bottle of wine we were warming to each other when the door opened. I didn't take much notice to begin with, but after my first kiss with Monique, I couldn't help but notice the two grinning faces that rose in unison above the partition. Dave Williams and Joe Higgins had become close friends that year, but both had a wicked sense of humour. Needless to say, I was the butt of their jokes for several months.

Monique was not only tall, she was also extremely fit and had agreed to a date because I could speak French and looked as though I could go the distance. I can safely say my experiment to tire myself out failed though no lack of effort on my part.

I didn't make the cut that week and to be honest I can't say I was sorry. Walking round like the living dead may have suited Dracula, but it was beginning to take its toll on me. And the comments from the boys were starting to wear thin. I was glad my experiment had proved to be flawed and I could move back to more orthodox methods.

Chapter 9
Tom Watson

For the rest of the season I decided to have a break from travelling and restricted myself to local events. I won a series of 6 pro ams and finished first in two important regional events that meant I won the South of England PGA order of merit. Apart from the cheques I picked up, I further subsidised my income by playing challenge matches against other pros. My teammate was Peter Hollington, who by this time had ditched his teacher and was the perfect four ball partner. He would play dreadful golf for a few holes, lulling our opponents into thinking they were playing against one man, and then produce a flash of brilliance to stun them.

Whilst Peter had lost his consistency, he had lost none of his competitive instinct and I delighted in watching him fight. There were none better and it was through his example I learned not to abandon a lost cause. A major contributing factor to us being able to grind out victories was that we often played for more cash than we carried and couldn't afford to lose.

One particular match we were four down with five to play and in danger of losing a record amount of money. It was like red rag to a bull for Peter, the harder the better as far as he was concerned. But even I couldn't believe it when he increased the bet. Peters first instinct was to bite off more than you can swallow, then chew bloody quickly.

'What the hell did you do that for?' I asked as we walked off the tee.

'We can do this Hoski, one hole at a time - just make sure you birdie this one.'

It was like Butch Cassidy and the Sundance Kid taking on the Bolivian army - plenty of bravado, not much to back it up with and I braced myself for annihilation.

Under Peter's instruction we embraced the challenge, fought the battle one hole at a time and against the odds we birdied the last five holes to win on the 18th. It was amazing to achieve something I had thought impossible and it was to prove an invaluable lesson.

You learn things from playing sport that can help in other walks of life, which as we all know is full of ups and downs. If you can learn to roll with the punches in a sporting environment, it makes it a lot easier to face adversity when it inevitably confronts you sometime in your life. I'd stood in front of thousands and taken beatings. Yet, I'd played in front of thousands and been applauded. I'd tasted both defeat and success and I had learned to take disappointment and not give up.

When the 1981 season was coming to a close I met some old school friends at a party who had just spent three years at university. I still considered myself a young kid on tour, but after talking to them, I realized that I'd grown up quite a bit. I seemed to be worldlier than they were. My friends were looking round for jobs but even with good degrees they were finding it tough. Although I had not had as much success as I would have liked, after talking to my friends I decided my years as a professional had not been a complete waste of time and it spurred me to carry on in golf.

****

As insurance against a season devoid of European Tour competition, I took my tour card in November. Out of a field of three hundred hopefuls, including Ian Woosnam, who was living in a camper van eating tins of beans to save money, I was one of fifty successful players. Combined with local events, it guaranteed me plenty of playing opportunities the following year and in preparation; I spent four months in the gym and hit balls everyday on the practice ground at Home Park.

After winning a few local events in the spring, which put some money in the bank, I travelled abroad to Sardinia for the Italian Open. The only way to get there was to have an overnight stop in Rome and fly on from there the next day.

For our stopover in Rome, Randy Fox, the travel coordinator, put me down to share with an American pro who had come across to Europe to experiment on our tour. His name was Mac O'Grady and he proved to be exceptional in every way. Highly intelligent, profoundly intense with a strong leaning towards Eastern philosophy, he knew more about the golf swing than anyone I had come across and for the next month I was utterly mesmerised by his capabilities. His knowledge of the swing was communicated in almost mathematical terms, so scientific was it, and he preached the theories of Homer Kelly and the 'Swing Machine'. Over a decade later, I was fascinated to see he had become associated with Ballesteros as his 'guru'.

Mac was a law unto himself and his way of assessing situations set him apart. On the key to playing good golf he once said, 'You must attain a neurological and biological serenity in chaos. You cannot let yourself be sabotaged by adrenaline.'

However, it was not his philosophising that impressed me, rather his striking ability. Several years after playing in Sardinia, Mac won on the US PGA Tour and when a survey was carried out amongst the top players asking who was the best striker in the world, Ballesteros and Watson had no hesitation in nominating O'Grady. He really was that good.

When I shared a room with him in Sardinia however, no one had heard of him and when we wandered down to the practice ground the morning after we arrived, I had no idea what to expect. The only other player practicing was Bobby Clampett, also a Homer Kelly pupil, but not a true convert according to Mac. He set about showing me the difference.

Pure and simple he was a genius when it came to hitting a golf ball. There wasn't a shot he hadn't mastered and his power was awesome. After a demonstration of his own brilliance, he added to the display when he mimicked the swing of every great golfer I had heard of. One by one, with absolute precision, he imitated the swings of Watson, Nicklaus, Trevino and his Hogan fade was as accurate as the original. To make the practice session legendary he pulled a left hand iron from his bag and went through the routine as a 'lefty'.

During the exhibition, we were joined by another pro. He watched the private show with the same awe as myself and when Mac left, after watching me hit balls for an hour, we chatted about what we had witnessed. Nick Mitchell became my closest friend on tour.

I practiced and played with Mac for the next month, during which I learned a great deal about the swing. Some of it I tried to incorporate into my own game, but the greatest benefit came from watching him mimic other players. It seemed so simple just to copy someone else's swing and it was a method I would shortly use myself.

Before Mac returned to the States he gave me a signed copy of the book, The Swing Machine, that his wife had brought across from California. A message written in the front complimented me on my knowledge of the swing, which I took as a great compliment as Mac didn't suffer fools gladly. My time with him helped me further my knowledge of the golf swing and at the time, I guess, I was about ninety percent of the way to understanding the golf swing in its entirety. The last ten percent took me another ten years.

After meeting Nick Mitchell, travelling away to play golf was a completely different proposition. If we played in a tournament we shared a room, so not only did that save on hotel bills but it meant I had a friend on tour.

We had both been fascinated by Mac O'Grady in Sardinia, and I had been particularly interested in the concept of mimicking golf swings. It seemed such a simple way to play golf. Rather than constantly search for the Holy Grail, you could simply stand up and copy your favorite player. One day, about a month later at the Welsh Classic, I asked Nick to watch me hit shots while I tried to imitate my hero Tom Watson. I found it quite easy to copy Watson because of his distinctive rhythm and after a few shots Nick complimented me on my version.

'You should try using it,' he said.

What started as a joke soon became my method. But what finally persuaded me to go for the complete Watson metamorphosis, was watching him win the U.S. Open at Pebble Beach. It was enough to make me put my personal theories on hold and simply copy the best. My friends couldn't believe it, a change in everything; rhythm, technique, and even clothes; Watson being a convert to the cardigan.

In the third round of the German Open I played with Sam Torrance and when I stood on the tee, carried out my Watson waggle and let rip, I heard him laugh; 'Jesus, thought it was Tom,' he said afterwards.

Not only did my shot making improve, but with the positivism that encapsulated Watson's game, no adversity seemed to affect me. The only problem was on the greens, where I became ludicrously attacking. But there were no half measures in my approach and I accepted the occasional three-putt with grace. In Germany I finished in the top twenty.

In Holland the following week, I blitzed my first two drives out of bounds and started with a nine, but employing my Watson walk, and his positivism, I carried on and simply ignored the disastrous start. I recovered to make the cut shooting a cracking sixty-nine in the second round.

In the back of my mind I felt I was somehow cheating the system, circumnavigating the problem of finding the solution to my natural swing, but it was a great relief not to be eternally absorbed in technique, and gave some credence to my father's theory that I had been suffering from paralysis through analysis.

Back home in local events my Watson swing cleaned up, but over the weeks I noticed I was becoming prone to a nasty pull hook.   With reasonable results I held back from delving too deeply into the reason why; I just leapt onto the tee, waggled, hit and bobbed merrily after the ball. One day however, as I was preparing for the German Open, the simplicity of that approach finally came to an end.

I was standing on the practice ground with Paul Way when a man representing a video company sauntered across, carrying the latest camera. At the time they were pretty rare and I had never seen my swing on tape. After chatting for awhile, he asked me if I would like to see my swing on the playback machine in the clubhouse.   Excitedly I fired off a few of my Watson swings and within minutes I was watching my swing for the first time. I was shattered. This was not Watson, this was someone trying to look like him and not doing a great job! Watson was far more upright, more inside on his attack onto the ball, with much less wrist cock at the top.

Looking back I should have been pleased; the rhythm was spot on, the overall action pretty competent, but it was not how I envisaged it and I was devastated. I could see where the occasional pull came from. My shoulders were spinning open too fast on the downswing throwing my attack onto the outside.

After watching my action for well over half an hour, I walked out of the clubhouse feeling dreadful. My swing was so different to how it felt. Up to that point of the season I'd played quite well, but in my warped mind that didn't matter. What did matter was swinging as I wanted to. It was like thinking you look like Arnold Schwarzenegger only to find you look like Mr Puniverse.

Immediately I embarked on a method of trying to swing the club more on the inside on the downswing, which would theoretically stop my pull. Nick understood my reasoning but thought it crazy for me to try a dramatic change mid season considering my successes. But by the time I teed it up in the European Open at Sunningdale, I was consumed with sorting out the problem.

On Thursday, first round of the event, the escapade came to a head. Standing on the eighth tee, a short par three, a typical hole where my pull might emerge, I made my Watson swing but through sheer physical effort, I held the club on the inside coming into impact. The result? The only shank I ever hit as a professional. The ball came right off the hosel and flew away at forty-five degrees to the right. On most courses it would've been lost, but the seventh hole runs at right angles to the eighth at Sunningdale and my ball disappeared over the trees and ended up on the down slope of the adjacent fairway.

My caddie was stunned and so was I when I realised what faced me. Playing behind was Sandy Lyle and my ball had come to a stop near him. Thousands of spectators lined the fairway and watched as I made my way across to play the shot.

"Morning Sandy" I said as I tried to work out where the green was, as it was considerably higher than where we were standing. There was a sea of spectators directly on my line, but they couldn't move, as the group on the ninth tee were about to hit off. It would have meant waiting an eternity for them to clear and I felt I had kept Sandy waiting long enough. I elected to hit over their heads and play the shot semi-blind.

Although I was scared stiff of another shank and a possible lawsuit if my ball hammered into the crowd, miraculously my ball found the green. I went on to complete the hole in four, but the tee shot badly affected me and it heralded a return to technique. I'd taken Tom as far as he could go and if I wanted to get better, it had to be through improving my own action rather than copying someone else's.

This was an important lesson I learned. Seeing yourself on film can be a great help for a golfer, but it's worth remembering that you will probably look very different to how you imagined. If you do want to improve and are keen to watch your own swing – be prepared for an X certificate showing. There are some real horror shows out there!

Chapter 10
The Tour Goes All-Exempt

In the winter of the 82/83 season I couldn't face a return to green keeping and with the opportunity of helping to teach football at my parents school in Northampton I spent the months travelling back and forward up the Ml. Occasionally one of the classroom teachers would be ill and I would stand in to help. I've experienced some pretty daunting things over the years but looking after the second form, a group of twenty five ten and eleven year olds, rates way up there on the order of merit. I used to drive home exhausted.

By this time I had met my future wife Vanessa and 'home' was her flat in Twickenham. When I returned from my daily trips to Northampton she used to think it hilarious that young children could shatter me when I could stand on the practice ground for hour upon hour without batting an eyelid. Certainly my estimation of teachers went up and another 'alternative' career was crossed off the list.

Vanessa and I had met at a pub in Richmond and we were as different as chalk and cheese. I was impulsive, headstrong and fanatical, she, laid-back, methodical and content. Long term I hoped the maxim 'opposites attract' would work, but more than a decade later the theory proved wrong. We always got on well and even now, though separated, remain friends, but there was always something missing - on reflection, probably me.

Looking back I think my frequent trips away hid the potential problem. However at that time not only was I earning a regular income but I was playing well locally and for the first time I could remember I decided to take a long break from playing every week. Throughout 1983 I worked hard at the school and incredibly managed to store up some money in the bank, but as the year came to an end I started to miss the excitement of the tour.

The previous year there had been an influx of new pros playing the circuit and I had become friends with many of them. Golfers like Richard Boxall, Robert Lee, Mark Roe and Andrew Murray had come onto the scene and not only were they good at golf; they were all very bright guys. I would have paid money to hear Richard tells jokes at the back of the tour bus.

It had also been the year when Ian Woosnam had broken in the Italian Open in Sardinia, the same week I had met Mac O'Grady. Suddenly one of our 'band of brothers' had shot to world fame and we were thrilled. It was watching Woosnam's rise in the world of golf, as much an anything, that persuaded me to return to playing more golf in 1984. As 1983 came to a close I entered the tour school, managed to win a card for the following season and started to work very hard at my game.

Throughout the winter my game improved. I kept a detailed diary of all my swing thoughts and my increasing knowledge led me to understand the 'secret' of my game was hidden in the murky area usually described in books, 'and the wrists cock naturally half way in the backswing'. Well, they didn't with me (not with any accuracy), nor for ninety-nine percent of all golfers, and anyone who opts for that over a simplified explanation is copping out.

I may not have been able to swing the club naturally through the correct position but I did know where the club should be when the wrist cock had been completed and this gave me two options. First I could actually stop half way back giving myself time to check my position, a method I employed in the Lawrence Batley in 1982, (to the amusement of my playing partner Neil Coles). Alternatively I could slow down my swing on the way back so I could control it inch by inch, virtually placing it into the correct slot but without an actual pause. Although highly unusual in its lack of speed, and that I was sacrificing full power for accuracy, it was the latter method I decided to adopt for the 1984. As April approached I carried on working at the school but couldn't wait to get back to tournament golf.

But a month before travelling to the first event disaster struck. I ripped an Achilles tendon tackling an over large fourteen-year-old and was laid up for two months. When the tour started I was hobbling around on crutches.

Throughout my career I had been lucky enough to remain injury free and I couldn't have picked a worse time for an enforced lay off. After some ten events the tour officials decided to make the circuit all exempt for the 1985 season. No longer would there be an opportunity to pre-qualify, the top hundred and twenty players from the previous year's order of merit, would make up the fields. It was a decision that has affected the amount of English players coming through the ranks and if, in years to come, the Ryder Cup team is made up mainly of continental pros - the reason lies in the introduction of all exempt tour.

Before 1985 there were always a few places available in pre-qualifying for aspiring young pros to earn a place in the main event. Once in, they could match their games against the best and gain a crucial insight into the standard required to make it on tour. The likes Ian Woosnam, Peter Mitchell and Barry Lane, all future tournament winners, gained invaluable experience in this way.

In America, abandoning pre- qualifying worked because an established 'second' tour was already in existence. In England however, young players who didn't get on the all-exempt tour were limited to playing pro-ams on the regional PGA circuits. A secondary tour called the Challenge Tour had been set up, but out of twenty events, nineteen were abroad. The prize funds were much smaller than the main tour but the travelling expenses were the same. It was a quick way to get into big debt. The Challenge Tour was predominately for young pros lucky enough to have good sponsorships.

By the time the controversial mid season decision had been made in 1984 I had missed the early events and was playing 'catch up'. There was a race on for our futures and having missed the early events, I was in last place.

Fully recovered by early August I travelled away for the German Open, where my slow controlled backswing enabled me to shoot 68 in the last round when I played with Jamie Crow, arguably the world's longest player. Full of enthusiasm and undaunted at being out driven by fifty yards on every hole, the following week I headed for the European Masters in Switzerland and the spectacular venue of Crans-sur-Sierre.

Over the last couple of seasons I had played in some fantastic places, Biarritz, Monte Carlo, Cannes, Rome, but the course at Crans Montana is simply breathtaking. Perched high up at over five thousand feet, the Crans course is surrounded by mountains and valleys, making it the most scenic venue on tour, but more importantly to me it was a course that suited my game.

Shorter than the usual tour courses and coupled to the thin air at altitude (in which the ball travels further) I was able to reach all the holes using only ninety percent power. For once I was almost on equal terms.

I shot a good 68 the first day and with little else to do in the small town of Crans, I wandered round the course in the afternoon to watch how a world-class player negotiated the test.

The Swiss federation traditionally imported a famous American to add prestige to the event and that year, fresh from his second place in the USPGA, it was Lanny Wadkins. Nowadays the top Americans hold no greater 'aura' than the likes of Woosie, Faldo, and Lyle etc. but at the time they were the best. It was an experience to see such a great player crunch his way round. He took huge divots, particularly with his short irons and whilst not the longest player his driving was exceptional, placing the ball in the right spot, on every fairway.

Wadkins was known to be one of the fiercest competitors on the U.S. tour and if he had a weakness it was his putting. Only the week before, I'd seen it let him down when watching the battle between himself and Trevino for the PGA on television. It was rumored he'd been attracted to the European Masters by a great deal of appearance money and I could almost feel the hero worship of the crowds as he gritted his way around. Striking the ball superbly he ended up shooting 67 and it was a privilege to watch the star.

After I'd made the cut on Friday, for different entertainment, I took the cable car from the back garden of our hotel to the summit of the Sierre Mountain. Never having been exposed to great heights it was the first time I realised I suffer from vertigo. The cable car that travels up the Sierre Mountain is unusually high up off the ground (so I've been told) and when I eventually got off at the top my knuckles were white through hanging on to the sides. But it was worth it. As I stood on the summit the sense of freedom was unforgettable and even though it was bitterly cold, with snow on the ground, I stayed for quite some time soaking up the experience. With an aversion to confined spaces it gave me the most intense sense of physical freedom. I knew that should I never have the opportunity again, I would always have the memory.

As soon as I returned to the hotel the phone rang - it was Nick from the course; 'Hoski, have you heard the draw?' he asked referring to the teeing off times of the next day.

'No - got mine?'

"Yeah, eleven o'clock, you're playing with Lanny Wadkins.'

It was the first time I was to play with a really famous American and I was both thrilled and apprehensive at the same time.

When I arrived at the course the following morning there was hardly a spectator to be seen on the course and I realised why as I walked to the practice ground. They were all waiting for Lanny (and me) on the first tee. It was packed and even an hour before we were due on the tee spectators were queuing four deep to see their hero. I went off to practice, warmed up on the putting green and after an eternity we were called to the tee.

'Morning Lanny' I said shaking hands with the man known not to suffer fools gladly. 'Glad to know you John' he said, and I realised he knew my name before being told. I don't care how, but he knew!

In Switzerland there are no ropes to hold back the gallery, the spectators walk with you and when Lanny (and I) headed down the first, two thousand spectators followed. As we passed the putting green I saw my friends watching us go, 'Go gettum Hoski' they called. It was a treat for anyone to play with the star attraction and I knew my friends were hoping I could put up a good showing.

We probably held the two ends of the spectrum with regards to technique. Wadkins had one of the fastest swings on tour, literally shooting from the hip - I had probably the slowest backswing in world golf! But undaunted by appearing unorthodox I stuck to my guns. On the first hole, a par five, I slotted a twenty five foot putt for birdie and the crowd, almost pressing onto the putting green made a huge roar as the ball disappeared. Lanny made a par.

I hit two good shots onto the lawn of the second hole and from ten feet holed for another birdie and another huge round of cheering. I hadn't played in front of such a large crowd before and the atmosphere was exhilarating. It seemed every move I made was scrutinised by the gallery and it was rather self-consciously I smiled at the spectators thanking them for the encouragement.

The third hole is a relatively tight par three, normally a five iron but in both the previous rounds

I had found the traps. Deciding therefore to hit more club, I 'smoothed' a four iron. The ball took off true and straight, landed in the middle of the green and rolled to no more than five feet from the hole. When the putt went in for my third birdie on the trot the sound of cheering was deafening and although I tried to look as though it was commonplace for me to produce such amazing feats, I couldn't help but grin.

After years of struggling I was tasting success on the course and, for once, I felt I should be there, not locked away like some embarrassing relative. As I walked to the forth tee I knew that if the wheels were going to come off it would be there. The forth was the toughest hole on the course requiring a fade off the tee, followed by a long iron to a partially hidden target. My drive went according to plan but I caught my four iron slightly thin and it finished on the front portion of the green some sixty feet short of the pin which was at the back. It was a tricky putt, several slopes had to be negotiated and to get the ball within three feet would have been an achievement, but that day it didn't matter. My ball, homing in on the cup like an Exocet missile found the hole and when it dropped, the crowd went berserk. Four birdies in four holes - surely it couldn't last?!

When my putt went in from twenty feet at the next to record my fifth consecutive birdie the noise from the appreciative crowd was almost physical and my spine tingled with almost orgasmic satisfaction.

'Boy you sure know how to use this thing,' said Lanny as he looked at my putter on the sixth tee.

It was a 'trip' that no chemical could induce, an adrenaline 'fix' unforgettable in it's' quality and the memory was imprinted into my physical makeup and became the template I would strive to recapture for years.

I reached the turn in thirty-one, lowest nine of the week and on the back nine I faced a different sort of pressure than I was used to. Rather than trying to 'hang on', this time I was trying to go more under par, but perhaps I tried too hard or simply ran out of luck, but I made one or two errors and completed the round in 69. Lanny however seemed to shift into top gear after the front nine and with the help of two holed wedge shots for eagle (which took the gallery to new heights of ecstasy), he completed the round in sixty four.

When the round finished he invited me in for lunch and for an hour we chatted about his life and mine. Contrasting? Certainly. But it was Lanny and I together and for once I'd earned respect. Very different from the Turnberry days.

While I came to learn in my career that no one round is important in itself, when I reached the final event of the year I needed to finish in the top twenty to gain a card on the all exempt tour. I was paying the penalty for missing out the first half of the season. I made the cut in the Portuguese Open and in the last round playing with Tommy Horton I needed to shoot a sixty-seven to achieve my target.

Trying to shoot a particular score is never the best way to approach competitive golf and when disaster came at least I was put to the sword quickly. On the eighth hole at Quinta do Lago, a long par five, I was standing at two under par but I hooked my tee shot going for a big drive and the ball ended up in the trees. I should have stayed calm accepted the situation and taken my medicine but I felt I had to make good distance with my recovery shot to be able to hit the green in three. At impact I kept my head down but the immediate sound of the ball ricocheting off timber signified a failed attempt at extricating myself. It seemed my career was to remain in the trees with my ball.

Life is about making decisions - sometimes you make the wrong one. Certainly I shouldn't have gambled quite so extravagantly on my recovery shot, but at the time I couldn't see the wood from the trees.

Later that night, having a feeling that my golf career had ended I sat in a small bar with Barry Lane and Dave William's, two old friends, reflecting on the season. Barry was to shortly win $1,000,000 in the WGC match play. Dave was to become one of the top rules officials on tour. For me – I had no idea what the future held.

Chapter 11
Bond – James Bond

When I returned to England I had plenty of time to think and reflect about lost opportunities. I had been so close, just some four hundred pounds short of the mark, but close was not good enough and I faced an uncertain future.

During my days of reflection I happened to bump into a member of Home Park Golf club who was the manager of a local branch of the Abbey Life insurance company. Whilst playing an early morning round he listened to my dilemma suggesting I might try a change of career to his profitable industry. Certainly, the financial security that a successful insurance agent could carve out attracted me, but were all my golfing years going to go to waste?

After discussing my reservations I agreed to go to his office for an interview and the following week, I turned up to his Hounslow branch for the mandatory personality test. Half an hour of quick fire questions produced a graph. Sitting down over coffee, he interpreted it.

'The bottom line is, you're great at motivating people, lousy at closing the deal.'

I was amazed the test could reveal such an accurate picture, particularly as I had tried to fool it, aware I had one or two weaknesses. What he said next shocked me. 'Basically you're three under after fourteen holes, you finish off three over. Even though the results suggested I would struggle to survive in the cut-throat world of selling insurance, pensions and saving plans, he took me on and within a week I found myself in Bournemouth for product training and a roll playing selling course. Define the need - sell the benefit - close the sale.

Defining the need was no problem; I was great at analysis. Selling the benefit was easy; I had come top of the product knowledge tests and knew every plan backwards. But could I close?!

In roll playing I was fine, but when it came to real life I would have the customer eating out of my hand, pen poised above the cheque book, but I would still feel compelled to give them an 'out'. Apparently, I had no killer instinct. 'Take your time and think about it,' my natural reaction.

The more I pondered on this weakness, the more I realised it was a reflection of the way I compiled a golf score. All too often I had played myself into a good position, glaringly with Lanny Wadkins the previous year, only to let the score slip away over the closing holes.

I had been aware that 'finishing' hadn't been my forte but assumed the main reason was pressure affecting my swing and had sought an impregnable action. However, this new insight showed my incapability in a new light - perhaps it was the mind that needed strengthening rather than the swing.

Inevitably, I failed to take the financial world by storm and with my career options running out, and still doing everything possible to avoid London, I was spurred on to concentrate on the local tournaments where I could earn enough to pay the bills.

Just being aware that problems were liable to arise on the last few holes was not enough to stop them. In fact if anything, it was inviting disaster, content my new theory was proving correct as my ball slammed into the trees. But I tried to stick to a more disciplined attitude over the closing holes and after winning several small tournaments was delighted with my successes. I longed though to try out my new method in the cauldron of tour pressure and was thrilled, in early May, when I was given a place in the PGA Championships at Wentworth.

In practice I had a surprising boost when Sandy Lyle asked if he could join me, the inevitable crowd giving a taste of much needed match pressure. However, after a relatively long time away from tour golf, my slow swing did not reflect the lay off and I played surprisingly well. It was all rather enjoyable and for a fleeting moment I considered trying to sell Sandy a pension plan!

Having played well in practice it was really annoying that in the first three rounds of the Championship I played myself into good positions and blew it every time. For the last seven holes of the second round I was covered by the BBC cameras and later, when I watched my performance on video, it clearly showed how my routine changed when confronted with the pressure of the closing holes. I speeded up, rushed decisions and when I faced a particularly difficult shot on at the sixteenth, went into a blind panic.

'Take your time, take your time,' my father had been saying to me for years - I never had.

With only two holes to go in the event I was lying in thirtieth place and if I could finish well, a cheque for two thousand pounds waited for me, but the seventeenth hole at Wentworth is a tough test under pressure.

I pulled my tee shot into the left hand rough, thick and wet after the dreadful May weather and my second shot required a long, hooked shot. Not wanting to hit my third shot from below the crest of the hill, length was important. Pressing too much though, I over-turned the clubface at impact taking off all the loft. On take off the ball got tangled in the rough and only travelled five yards.

This was where I needed cool calm thinking, not the increasing panic that grabbed me. As the red mist descended, I played my next shot without a firm plan in mind. I struck the ball superbly, but this time failed to close the blade at all. For a fleeting second I saw the surprised expression on my father's face as my ball flew across the fairway, over his head, deep into the forest on the other side. I was stunned. Short of money, the cheque I had mentally banked was deflating by hundreds with every wasted shot.

I announced to Jose Rivero, my playing partner that I would play a provisional. I dropped a ball and hit the same club, but this time I reverted to my original mistake and only shifted the ball several yards. All mental control suddenly disappeared and I became about as calm as the waves in a mid Atlantic storm. A quick hack onto the fairway, followed by a rushed long iron and counting my expected two penalty shots I was lying seven; a chip and two putts for a ten. It looked as though I had blown everything.

Suddenly from out of the trees an official appeared.

'I think we've found it' he said. I felt sick and ran across the fairway to where he was pointing. Ignoring the pain of the brambles tearing my face and hands, I clawed my way into a clearing some forty yards in where an official was standing next to a ball. My ball! None of the shots I had hit with my provisional ball counted as I had hit them before reaching my original.

On scrutiny, not only was my ball sitting up on a lovely tuft of grass but miraculously I could also make a full swing. There was one escape route, a small hole in the ceiling of branches above me and I decided to take the shot on. At impact, I kept my head down listening for the sound of ball crashing into the branches but all I heard moments later was my father's strained voice shouting; 'It's out, it's out.'

Even though my ball had found the fairway I was still left with a blind shot of over two hundred yards from the green. Still managing to keep my swing under control my four iron came to a stop some four feet from the hole and with a rather nervy stroke, holed the putt for a par and the most incredible escape. Half an hour later, after making birdie on the last, I calculated I had won about £2000.

As I made my way home I knew I had been blessed with the luck of the devil on the 17th. My attitude had been dreadful in those few minutes when I needed to remain calm and I was determined to do something about it.

That night after diner, while my father was recovering from the stress, I told my mother about my great escape and how I had let myself down by not remaining calm.

'Showbiz darling,' said my mother who had trained at the Royal Academy and was at one with the performing arts. 'You'll just have to act calm, even though you may not feel it dear.'

Over the weeks the more I thought about it, the

more it made sense. I, John Hoskison, may not be able to remain calm but surely I could act like someone who did. I wanted the killer instinct; I wanted to remain cool under fire. There was one answer; Bond - James Bond. I had once copied the swing of one of my golfing heroes Tom Watson, so why not adopt the attitude of one of my literary heroes. It all made perfect sense.

For the next month I worked on my new identity, read every Bond book again, and by the time August came smoked Winston cigarettes (because of the gold ring on the filter), drank Martini cocktails (shaken not stirred), and bought myself two pairs of expensive sports slacks from a specialist London tailor.

My reward was unrivalled success in local tournaments and one or two good performances on the tour even to the extent of being awarded a 'shooting star' award for the most improved order of merit position.

In late August my performances on tour earned me a place in the Cannes Open - Bonds 'playground' and with Nick Mitchell also being exempt; we booked a flight and took off to the South of France. I wore a navy, double breasted blazer, cravat and straw Panama hat, Nick after seeing me, a grin from ear to ear.

My local success had swelled the coffers in the bank and to add to the luxury of our trip, rather than take the bus laid on for the players from Nice airport, we hired a two liter, fuel injection convertible Escort, black shiny and quick, but it was not me who drove. No expense had been spared and it was Ben, a friend of ours who chauffeured for the week. Our apartment, overlooking the harbour in Cannes was about as swish as we could afford and wandering down to one of the local restaurants, to sample the exquisite delicacies of Bond's favorite French cuisine – to all intents and purposes I was 007.

The tournament was played at the Cannes Mougins complex and to further add to the scene the sponsors, Martini, had a players tent where every conceivable concoction could be ordered.

'Shaken not stirred,' I specifically ordered from the waiter.

****

Bond remained cool and unflappable throughout the tournament. With consummate ease he made the cut using a slow backswing, but it was a deceptive action concealing an extra twenty yards of power when required. After three rounds Bond was lying in a position he had been in before, midway through the field in thirtieth place. But few could match the steely determination of the experienced agent in the final stretch.

Nick Mitchell had not made the cut and wandered out to watch Bond play the final six holes. There was a time in the past when Bond had wavered at this stage, but not this time. With Ben as his side kick they entered the final stretch with steely determination.

Birdies on fourteen and fifteen were achieved with ruthless precision on the greens, but it was the nerveless decision making of the agent on the sixteenth that reminded Nick Mitchell he was watching an assassin. The risk appeared suicidal, but with uncompromising commitment and a swing pulled from a textbook, Bond fired his three wood straight over the trees towards the heart of the green. The putt for eagle was a formality.

A solid par at the tricky seventeenth and Bond approached the eighteenth tee with the confidence of a veteran. 'Iron for safety?' asked Ben.

'Driver' said the agent with the hint of a grin.

Bond had a slow casual practice swing and then unleashed his drive bullet straight, bisecting the narrow fairway. The applause from the crowd was met with a cursory nod from Bond.

The wedge shot to the last green would have terrified less experienced men in the field, but Bond struck the shot with absolute precision. The ball took one bounce, landed some ten feet past the hole then to the amazement of the gallery, gripped and screwed back to within ten feet of the flag. The appreciative crowd clapped loudly as the agent walked to the green to confront the final hurdle; a treacherous downhill putt with a massive break from left to right.

Bond looked at the dangerous putt, which begged the ultimate question - attack or defend? Bond relished the challenge and with a jaw set with determination he prepared for the showdown.

The putt was struck perfectly but it was no lag and the crowd held their breath as the ball travelled fast towards the hole. Arcing gracefully across the slope it thumped into the centre of the cup and disappeared from sight. The crowd erupted. Five under for the last six holes, fifteenth in the tournament, and a healthy cheque.

Nick met Bond at the back of the green; 'That was incredible Hoski'. No kidding -I wondered who Hoski was.

With some money in the bank there was no way I was going back to England without taking a couple of days off. The next day we drove to Monte Carlo and the setting of Casino Royale. For two days we stayed in a hotel a stone's throw from the most famous casino in the world and displaying the discipline of professional gamblers played, and slowly won at roulette, finishing off with a six hour stint at Black Jack, Bonds' game.

It was life in the fast lane, literally, as Ben insisted on a few circuits in our black machine round the grand prix track before our departure from Nice airport. When we finally touched down in England I knew I had carved out a memory, so deep it would live with me always; as sure as 'Diamonds are Forever'.

Chapter 12
West Surrey

When I returned to Britain from the Cannes Open I decided not to go to the tour school. There was no need. I had played only a handful of events that season finishing in an almost identical position in the order of merit to the previous year, and there was no reason but to expect the same starts in 1986.

To my horror, when the new schedule was published in February events I expected to play in had either disappeared or been moved to other parts of the season. The Cannes Open, virtually the last event in 1985 became the first in 1986 when all the players were fresh and eager to play making the fields full - no space for me.

Overnight I was condemned to earning my living from local events. Bond was far too expensive to represent me locally (he had very exotic tastes) and with only small purses available in pro ams, my long-term future in the world of golf was looking decidedly dodgy.

I was already looking around for another job to supplement my income, when my parents took the plunge and invested their spare capital in an ambition they'd nurtured for years. They bought a wine bar. Ever since discovering Charcos in Chelsea, after one of my sister's performances at the Albert Hall, they'd wanted their own, and what's more, to run it on similar lines; classical music and only serving wine. To keep the venture in the family my father offered me the job of helping to run Valentines in Cranleigh and after discussing the move with Vanessa, we grabbed the opportunity. In late July we moved into the flat above the wine bar, eight miles south west of Guildford.

The wine bar was beautifully decorated and the venture would have been a massive success in London, but Cranleigh was not a place that could adapt to the 'no larger' concept. It may well be the largest town in England, but it's a cultural desert. Pinot Noire and Bach were a hard act to sell and I started to panic the venture would never take off.

One night, sitting in the quiet bar waiting for a customer to come in, I noticed an advertisement in Golf Illustrated advertising the position of club professional at West Surrey Golf Club, no more than six miles down the road. After discussing the move with Vanessa, I decided to apply for the job.

I compiled a good CV and sent it off confident I would get an interview, but after weeks of silence I gave up hope. Worried I'd put something in my CV that put off the club, I contacted a nearby professional who taught at the PGA school. When Roger Mace read my application he was surprised I had not received a reply and phoned up the chairman of West Surrey who he personally knew. A week later I was invited to a playing interview.

'To make you feel relaxed,' said the chairman, explaining the unusual format, but when I teed off, I felt I was playing for my future and was under more pressure than I could remember.

Having to be jovial and chatty at the same

time as showing off golfing prowess was a difficult combination, particularly as I had hardly played at all for six months, but somehow my swing stood up to the test and after completing the front nine in five under par, during which I had also cured the shank of one of my playing partners, I couldn't help feel the job was mine. The next day I was thrilled when offered the position, but feeling as though I was deserting a sinking ship, I announced the news rather sheepishly to my parents.

They accepted it with the same generosity that they'd always shown and I hoped that if I ever had a child I could be as kind and understanding. I must have been a disappointment to my parents. My sister had made it as a top violinist, my mother was a professional pianist and my father a top linguist. As teachers, there were none better. They'd done everything they could to support my ambition, but even though turning my back on a career as a competitive golfer, they were still only concerned with my happiness. As far as parents go I'd been dealt one hell of a hand.

Within a month of being offered the job I had moved into the pros shop at West Surrey. Initially I knew very little about being a club pro. At the interview I'd told the directors about my extensive teaching diary, yet I'd hardly taught any club golfers. I had told them about my fantastic ability at club repairs, however, I had only passed my PGA exams because the examiner happened to be the father of a close friend. During the practical test, when demonstrating my proficiency at club repairs, he had kindly turned away after I drilled straight through the head of the Macgregor wood I was trying to re-shaft.

After securing a bank loan, I ordered over

twenty thousand pounds worth of equipment from golf manufacturers and had it delivered to the shop. Trying to keep the costs down, I refitted and decorated the shop myself and at first, life was pretty hard. Without an assistant, I was responsible for all jobs; paying invoices, ordering goods, teaching and club repairs.

Finally I was earning an income I could rely on, but it was incredibly boring work and as the weeks progressed, I realised everything I was doing could have been done by anyone dragged off the street and given a few weeks training.

Yes, I was liked, a nice polite young man, but I wanted respect and the only way to earn that was to show the members I excelled at the game they loved. Even with my apparent good record, until I showed them something special, I would only be regarded as a glorified shop keeper.

In late summer 1987, only four months after starting my new job, the opportunity came. Every year in Great Britain the PGA stage a tournament open to all three thousand club professionals and, after qualifying, I headed to Manchester for the National Club Professional Championships.

Carrying my own bag in terrible weather, I shot 67 in the first round and was delighted. For the next two rounds I continued to play well and when the final round started, I was lying in second place, two shots behind Russell Weir, one ahead of David Huish. Several hundred spectators turned out to watch, including Peter Alliss, the famous commentator, who was to present the prizes at the completion of play. It was a real thrill to be involved in another competition, and fresh for a fight I clawed my way back to be level with Russell on the last hole. I hit a good shot to the par three, but a superb five iron to two feet resulted in a birdie for Russell and second place for me.

It was a nice tidy performance, a cheque for two thousand pounds, but more, much more, was the coverage I received in the national press; West Surrey's name always in tandem with mine. When I returned home the atmosphere in the shop had changed. People were falling over themselves to get in and congratulate me and at the end of the year, my results, and the publicity it attracted the club, led to a substantial salary increase.

Suddenly, what was proving to be a slightly boring job, turned out to be the best. To add to the respect my 1987 results earned me, the following summer I repeated the performance at Harlech in Wales. My third place was not only regarded as an achievement in itself, but it secured me a place in the PGA cup team that was to take on the Americans at the Belfry in July.

****

The PGA Cup is a bi-annual event and one of the most important in the calendar of the association. Also known as the mini Ryder Cup, the match is regarded as a dress rehearsal for its big brother the following year; the Ryder Cup itself. All the top ranking American officials come across and many of the European Tour hierarchy are present. The previous winter Vanessa and I had got married and at the time of the match, she was six months pregnant. Initially we debated whether she should make the trip, but when Phil Weaver, the chairman of the PGA heard, he insisted Vanessa came and arranged for her to have a buggy at her disposal so she could take a ride whenever she wanted. It was a gesture typical of the attention the players received that week, and it was mainly due to how Tony Jacklin had transformed the Ryder Cup team. If you wanted to win, you had to have a team that had bonded. When we arrived at the Belfry, the day after the Open Championship had finished, the complex was packed with rules officials, sponsors and organisers. We were also greeted with the unusual sight of two fire engines sitting on the eighteenth fairway, where the atrocious weather had led to an extension to the famous lake and the fairway was a foot under water.

For four days the team battled it out with our adversaries from over the pond; and they were good. Gibby Gilbert who had finished runner up to Ballesteros in the US Masters, Bob Menne, Tom Wargo and they were just the players I played against. Out of the ten players in our team, there were only two of us who were picked to play every match and by the end of the week I was knackered. Five rounds in three days had been tough, but my game had stood up well.

Representing your country as a professional sportsman involves more pressure than when you're just representing yourself, and it was a thrill being involved in an event that stimulated so much interest. The match had been extensively covered by the national press, and several times my name had been headlined as the driving force behind an attempted comeback. Unfortunately, the USA were too strong and we lost the overall match, but personally I had performed very well and had a fantastic time, making many new friends from the USA.

In my singles match on the last day, for the fourth time that week I played against Bob Menne. He'd won the Kemper Open on the PGA Tour only a couple of years before. He was long and he was bullet straight. It seemed half the members from West

Surrey had made the trip to Birmingham to watch the match.

When I reached the ninth hole, the match between the two sides was close and it looked as though the overall result might settle on the outcome of my game. It was raining, the wind was gale force but digging deeper than I have ever done before, I managed to birdie the 13th 14th and 15th to win 4&3. When the captain of my team came to congratulate me on the 15th green, I could barely contain myself. I remember my bottom lip trembling so much I couldn't say anything as I was so choked up with the effort and emotion. It was the most incredible experience.

I returned from the PGA Cup matches to a fantastic welcome. The local press had followed my progress over the week and members I hadn't seen for months came in to congratulate me on my individual performance. With so many bodies in the shop I was sitting on a gold mine. Wallets in hand they would come in looking to buy, and the trust I had built up over the previous months should have sent my takings through the roof. 'If John says it's good it must be good'. But I was no wheeler-dealer and definitely no salesman.

'Have a think and come back later,' I used to say. Not exactly the best closing line of all time! Or even worse, 'If you like it, take it now and pay later.'

Saying this I was in a difficult position. I was being paid the highest salary of all the local pros and as part of the package, a car from a local garage. I was also making cheques playing in local tournaments so when I was confronted with selling, I felt guilty at making a profit. Although many people would have given their right arm to work in such an environment, I never felt comfortable with the mechanics of the shop and decided to hire a team of assistants to manage the retailing, leaving me to play and socialise with the members.

In the winter of 88/89, after educating my 'team' on the virtues of politeness, service and selling, on the basis of do as I say, not as I do with regards to making sales, I bought myself a video camera and set about finding the missing link to my golf swing.

In the mornings I would go for a run, and be in the shop by nine o'clock, where I would spend an hour listening to any problems from the 'team', but who I paid exceptionally well not to have any. The rest of the day would be mine. With camera on tripod, I would wander out to the practice ground and work on my swing for hours, chatting to the members who came out to watch, often joining them for lunch. Occasionally, I would need to find out how my latest 'feel' would operate and I would venture out for a game with the members round the enchanting West Surrey course, for which I would be paid! The relationship that developed between the members and myself was unusually close and whilst it wasn't great for business, I regarded many of the members as friends.

When spring came I was looking forward to playing after a competitively dormant winter and I started off the season with a few local pro-ams in which I shot low scores managing to win most of them.

My life was absolutely idyllic. Vanessa and I now had a son.

My success in local events led to other playing opportunities and in late May I was invited to play in the Brian Taylor memorial, a European Tour pro-am at Sunningdale Golf Club, which was guaranteed money just for teeing it up. On a lovely sunny day in May I travelled to the event eager to try out my game on a top course.

Three amateur golfers joined me to make up the team and we set off happy, laughing and determined to get in the prizes. After sixteen holes we were in a great position. If we maintained our momentum over the last two, we were in with a shout of winning, but my amateur partners were starting to crumble under the pressure. I needed to take control and haul them over the line.

After a good drive on the seventeenth, I hit an attacking approach shot that took an unusually hard bounce and my ball finished up slightly over the green on the left side. No problem; the shot back was the sort of shot I had always been good at, but when I got to my ball it was lying in an old divot hole. Two of my partners were already out of the hole and they watched expectantly, hoping for me to produce something special. The shot however was much harder that it had initially appeared. Not only was the ball sitting down, but I had to hit the shot over the corner of a bunker and stop it quickly on the green.

Coming into impact I must have just lifted my head a fraction. Rather than the club sliding underneath the ball, the leading edge caught the bottom of it sending it flying across the green at lightning speed, where it disappeared into a bunker. It surprised me as much as my partners.

'Don't worry John, you'll hole the next one,' said Ronnie.

When I walked round the green I found my ball had run through the trap into an even worse lie than the one I had just played from. I kept my practice swing nice and smooth, but this time it was not simple mechanics that let me down. This time, as the club moved into impact, I felt my right hand 'twitch' and for the first time in twenty years I 'yipped' a shot. It was the most extraordinary sensation, as though my right hand had suddenly developed a personality of its own.

When I attempted my next shot back from the other side of the green, my right hand decided to 'speak' again. This time ball took off like a missile, almost hitting my playing partners, leaving them open mouthed in shock. From the heather I duffed my next shot into a bunker. It took me two further 'yippy hacks' to get the ball onto the putting surface. My partners didn't know what to say. For sixteen holes I'd been so consistent and then, the first time they had to rely on me, I'd blown everything with a ten.

We had lunch together after the round, but all I can remember is sitting at a table, head in hands, repeating, 'It's never happened before.' I had gone out for a pleasant walk in the country and had come back with Bubonic plague; I had caught the disease that is the nightmare of any professional.

For a month after the event, I remained in a daze while I tried to come to terms with a complaint that affected even the 'greats'. Langer, Snead, Watson had all encountered the terrible twitch and I tried not to think of the maxim 'once encountered the yips stay forever'.

My immediate hope that they might be temporary was quickly dispelled by atrocious displays in captain-pro matches. Rather than get better, they started to affect my whole game. Drives, iron shots, chipping and finally putting, all suffered when my right arm decided to explode. The astonishing unpredictability of the twitch left me a gibbering idiot on the course. I tried everything I could think of to help, but nothing seemed to work.

For two months I avoided any form of

competition, but in July it was the PGA Cup team reunion at the Club Professional Championships, which took place at Prince's Sandwich and I had to play. Having finished in the top three on my last two appearances, I turned up to as one of the favourites, but no one knew I was suffering from the yips.

Princes Golf Club is a windswept links course where the Open Championship had taken place in the past, and like Royal Birkdale it was a very tough test. With a prime teeing off time, there were lots of people round the first tee when it was my turn to drive, but all remained silent when my ball took off at forty five degrees. I found the shot, there are no trees at Prince's, but every shot from then on gave me nightmares. After two months of trying to pacify my offending limb, it grabbed the opportunity to embarrass me and started to twitch with the unpredictability of a severed electric cable. I fatted chips, fluffed pitches, thinned iron shots and topped drives. Every time I stood over a shot, I quaked with fear, and my smashed confidence was reflected in my scoring. After twelve holes I was eighteen over par.

The display utterly shocked my playing partners and on the thirteenth hole, unable to hit the green from thirty yards I had no alternative but to pick my ball up and walk in. I left my playing partners gazing after me, watching my departing shell stagger back to the clubhouse.

I listed injury as the reason for my withdrawal, the PGA don't recognize mental instability as an illness, and I feigned a shoulder problem to save myself a fine. When I drove back to West Surrey, shattered by the experience, I was aware that the end of my competitive career was nigh.

For the next year my form on the course

remains a blur of depression and experimentation. I tried every conceivable theory imaginable to overcome the problem but nothing I tried seemed to calm the explosive nature of my right hand as it came into impact. I even tried hitting shots with my eyes closed on the downswing to 'kid' my arm there was no reason to yip, but it had an intelligence of its own and nothing would fool it. Having cleaned up locally in events the year before, I finished last in the South Region order of merit, and with little option I basically gave up golf.

Occasionally I had to play with the members, it was part of my job description, but it was always a terrifying experience. No one could understand what I was going through and although I occasionally produced a good shot, simply on the law of averages, my general form on the course was terrible. By this time, Vanessa and I had brought a house in Godalming and were mortgaged to the eyeballs. It was not a good time to be suffering from my newly acquired disease.

In the spring of 1990 I was so short of money, that when one of my staff was offered a position of his own, I was quite happy to return to more duties in the shop and I gave up entering competitions.

However, there was one tournament I couldn't shy away from as everyone expected me to play; the National Club Professional Championships at Carnoustie. It was the tournament in which I had picked up my ball at Sandwich the previous year, and I drove to Scotland full of trepidation.

In the past, I would have looked forward to taking on the brutal links course where Hogan had dominated the Open in 1953. For years I'd heard stories about 'Hogan's Alley' and how he crushed the field of world class golfers. But rather than being able to enjoy the challenge, I was far too apprehensive about my form. Form the first tee to the last green it proved to be a complete nightmare.

There is no particular shot that stands out in my memory, just an overall impression of fear. Having tried to keep my twitch on a short rein for months, seeing an opportunity that was too good to miss, my right hand broke free of all constraints and repeatedly delivered hammering blows to my already fragile ego. By the time I reached the eleventh hole in the first round, I was nineteen over par. On the twelfth hole it started to rain. Not summer drizzle, but a really hard rain that soaked me, my clubs and my bag. Standing deep in the rough, after a wicked hook, I surveyed the surrounding scenery as if in some macabre surreal dream; the windswept dunes, the rain splashing down into puddles already lying on the ground. I could see the distant clubhouse beckoning through clouds of swirling moisture and far away, against a back drop of dark grey clouds, the church steeples in Carnoustie town.

It was as though my brain was taking in the final scene; a photograph of where it was all to end, where the golfer in me was to be laid to rest. When I walked off the course after the first round, part of my golfing soul remained on the Scottish links.

Chapter 13
No Hiding in The Open

Competitively broken by my Carnoustie experience, I spent the next twelve months working in the shop, teaching the members and generally hiding away from any form of competitive humiliation. My laurels were firmly rested to on former glories. Occasionally, I would venture onto the course to play a few holes, and it became apparent that I was liable to yip any shot that required less than full power. In captain pro matches the thrashed sand iron became my favorite shot.

Unfortunately, the members had started to become aware that I was hardly competing and one morning the secretary, Ralph Fanshawe, came into the shop.

'John, I was talking to some of the members yesterday, they said they were hoping to see you try to qualify for the Open this year.'

Just the thought sent a shiver through me. 'Where's it being played?' I asked. Since suffering from the yips, I had taken no interest in the world of golf.

'Royal Birkdale' he replied.

I almost burst out laughing with the irony. He was asking me to return to the scene of my greatest humiliation, but this time suffering with the yips. 'Some chance,' I thought. It would be professional suicide. My results over the last few years had gained me enough respect to remain at the top of the pile of local professionals. Shooting a couple of scores over 100 in the Open would do me no favours.

'Look Ralph, I'm a bit short of money at the moment and can't really afford to go.' I said. But Ralph was more than just a secretary; he was also a friend.

'I'm sure the members will help out. Even if they don't, I will. How much will it cost, about three hundred quid? It's just that we all miss the buzz you gave us in the PGA Cup match.'

I thought about it overnight, discussed it with Vanessa and eventually we decided I should make the effort. It was hardly much of a sacrifice to spend a couple of nights away playing the political game.

The next day, feeling like a charlaton, I explained I had no idea the members were so enthusiastic to see me play and I agreed to venture north. I couldn't accept Ralph's' kind offer though, not under false pretences. I had no intention of qualifying.

When July came, I travelled to Southport, scene of my biggest embarrassment as a professional. For company I took Andy, one of the lads from the shop who hadn't passed his PGA exams and as an amateur, he was able to caddie for me. He was thrilled by the prospect. 'Fool he' I thought.

We travelled up on Saturday morning, day before the first of my two qualifying rounds and when we arrived in Southport I found it had changed little over the years, except 'No Vacancies' hung in nearly every hotel. It was Open week and accommodation was tough to find.

Eventually we found a small guesthouse on the

outskirts of town and to keep expenses down, Andy and I shared a poky little room. I didn't bother with a practice round and instead wandered around the town telling Andy what had happened the last time I had played there. That night, after a pleasant meal, I slept peacefully.

On Sunday morning, after a leisurely breakfast we sauntered to Hesketh Golf Club, a short semi-parkland course, where I was to try to qualify. It was a beautiful morning, sunny, with hardly a breath of wind and the greens were perfect. Not giving two hoots about my score I twitched in a putt from sixty feet at the first for birdie. Without a care in the world my right hand remained relatively passive and I completed the front nine in level par.

On the tenth I hit a wicked pull into a deep bunker. I thinned the sand shot, but the ball hit the top of the trap, took one bounce and went into the hole. I holed two long putts on fifteen and sixteen and when I stood on the tee of the par-five seventeenth hole I was two under par. To entertain Andy I went for the green in two, but I thinned the ball and it took off quail high straight into the forest of trees. I had to smile as it went straight through the lot and scuttled onto the green. I finished the round in sixty-eight, not trying on a shot. That afternoon, instead of practicing, we spent time at the amusement park.

After another good night's rest, I woke early, packed my bag and checked out of the hotel knowing that in a few hours, we would be back on the motorway heading south. It was a beautiful day again and I was quite looking forward to having a casual walk in the sun.

Having played the tour, I was pretty experienced at gauging what score would qualify and I had decided to try to shoot 76, which would definitely miss, but would be considered a good try by my members.

When we teed up there was not a breath of wind and not a cloud in the sky. Playing golf when you don't want to score well is a frustrating business. Putts I hit too hard went in, risks I took came off and I found it all rather perturbing. However, there was always the seventeenth where I could shoot a ten if I needed it.

When I finally arrived at the penultimate hole, I needed to drop several shots to make sure I missed and as I pondered how to throw my score, the well-known TV comic Jimmy Tarbuck came onto the tee. I knew Jimmy from Coombe Hill, a course near my club, and he had wandered out to see me play.

The seventeenth hole requires an accurate drive and many players were hitting irons for safety. However, the most obvious way for me to drop shots was a wayward drive over the fence on the right, so in a gesture of feigned bravado, I pulled out my driver and gave the ball an almighty whack. I looked up expecting to see it shoot straight out of bounds, but watched in amazement as the bloody thing took off dead straight.

'Great shot,' said Jimmy.

'Shit' I thought.

Some sort of primeval instinct had taken over not allowing me to intentionally blow a score, but that didn't stop me from taking unnecessary chances. The risk I took with my next shot was ludicrous. I tried to carry the trees knowing that Seve was probably the only player who could have succeeded. Thankfully I heard my ball smash into the trees and was reaching for another when unbelievably I heard Jimmy shout out; 'It's okay, it's okay - it's on the green!'

My par on 17th meant I had to shoot an eight on

the last. I hammered my drive straight for the trap, but it ran over the edge. From out of a divot I played a suicidal three wood only to see the ball kick out of the bank of thick rough on the right straight onto the putting surface. I whacked the putt far too hard, but it hit the back of the hole, jumped into the air and came to a rest inches away. After tapping it in I walked off the course appalled that I hadn't the guts to throw my score.

Fortunately, after taking a look at the leader board all the good players still on the course and my score of 143 would still probably miss. After saying goodbye to Jimmy, we slung our gear into the car and got ready for the drive back home, but as we were pulling out of the car park Andy tapped me on the shoulder; 'Look over there,' he said. I stopped the car and looked in the direction he was pointing. It was like a scene from a biblical tale. The darkest weather front I had ever seen was moving in from the sea and within half an hour Armageddon had started. The rain hammered down and the wind blew up to gale force. The storm lasted three hours, and disastrously, play continued throughout. Ryder Cup player Paul Way shot 85 and many of the best players were literally blown away. Several hours later we drove back to the club, along the rain soaked roads, to find out that catastrophically my score had finished in the top three. I had qualified to play in the Open Championship at Royal Birkdale, scene of my worst nightmare.

'Good God' I thought realising what I was about to take on. 'There's no hiding in the Open.'

The next day, after a sleepless night, I turned up to the Championship venue, received my players badge and sat in the locker room contemplating practice, or suicide. All the players were allocated a locker for the week and when I opened mine, I found over twenty good luck telegrams from well-wishers. I had phoned the shop that morning to be told the 'buzz' at West Surrey was incredible. Apparently a deafening roar had erupted the night before, when my result had shown on Ceefax.

'Hoski,' came a voice that brought me out of my daydream. I looked up to see Dave Williams, a close friend from my tour days.

'Got a teeing off time at ten thirty - join me?'

If I had to go out for a round at least it could be with someone I knew, so I agreed. Half an hour later I stood on the tee with Andy, surrounded by hundreds of spectators.

'Hi John,' came a loud voice. I looked up to see a member from West Surrey waving at me from the stands. 'We're all here to watch you,' he called. Fortunately 'all' meant his wife and two sons, not the whole of West Surrey, but I knew they would be the first of many. Everyone had been so proud of me over the last few years. Okay, I was no world-beater, but I had played in the PGA Cup and knew the members would often say to their friends, 'but we've got John Hoskison as our club pro'. Well they wouldn't be boasting when I was known as the pro that'd shot the worst ever score in the Open.

When it was time to tee up to start our round, I had a practice swing that felt half decent, but when I went to hit the ball my right hand went into spasm. The ball came right off the toe of the club, and shot off at forty-five degrees, just missing the stand packed with spectators.

'Hit another,' said Dave smiling. I tried to look casual as Andy threw me a ball. My next shot was even worse and smashed into the stand just missing one of the crowd. When I walked off the tee I was trembling.

I dropped a ball in the middle of the fairway some two hundred yards from the green, well away from the ropes where spectators gathered, but I caught the four iron so heavy the ball only travelled forty yards. After completing the first hole I turned to Andy, 'I'm going to try to shoot a score, make me concentrate better.'

My dreadful striking continued though, and when I reached the end of the sixth hole, I was about ten over par. 'Any ideas?' I said to my bewildered caddie.

'You could try playing stableford,' he said. 'You might get a few points that way.' It was meant to be light humour, but it was too close to the truth.

Playing Royal Birkdale in front of so many people was the ultimate stage for my 'twitch', and over the course of the round, every time I went to swing my right had detonated with awesome results. My approximate score at the end was 94!

Dave was no longer smiling; he was genuinely embarrassed. Andy and I were both shattered.

'See why I didn't want to play?' I said to my young assistant as we walked off the eighteenth.

'What about some practice?' he said thinking it might help.

I couldn't think of anything worse and I smiled at the innocence of the non-afflicted. But to appease him we hitched a lift on one of the buggies that were transporting players to the practice ground. Our driver was a lunatic and at one point I almost fell off, but minutes later we arrived in one piece. Andy went to collect a bucket of balls and I found a bay at the far end away from all the spectators.

While I was trying to look professional having

a few practice swings, one of the golf equipment reps sauntered across, chatted for a while and eventually asked which manufacturer I was representing throughout the week.

'No one at the moment,' I replied. The least of my problems was finding someone to equip me. 'They'd probably sue anyway' I thought. But after much persuasion, I agreed to the reps proposition and signed a contract with Titleist. I was to be supplied with; a tour bag (only slightly smaller than my house), the latest Goretex waterproofs, top of the range leather shoes and a full range of Titleist Tour clothes. All of the equipment I planned to give Andy. It was the least I could do, knowing my intended plan.

While the rep went to arrange the equipment, I hit a few balls. I warmed up with some thrashed short irons, the only shots I trusted, but then decided to test my nerve with a few half-wedge shots off tight lies. I wanted to find out what was likely to happen in the most extreme circumstances. Everything felt fine right until impact, but then my legs stiffened, my head dropped and my right hand twitched as though it had been blitzed by 24,000 volts. The divot I gouged out flew forward almost as far as the ball. It must have looked as though I was practicing some sort of special trick shot.

Embarrassed by the awful chunks I was taking I started trying to clip shots clean off the top of the grass, but that proved impossible and I caught every ball thin. Had I been pitching to a green, they would have kneecapped anyone standing at the back, and it didn't bode well for playing on the course.

Abandoning both methods I decided on a confidence boosting exercise and tried to hit a few balls off a high tee peg. It would have looked pretty strange had anyone been close enough to see, but away from the spectators I could get away with it. I was just preparing to hit another when Andy spoke out.

'Hoski, look who's coming.' I turned my head to see Lee Trevino walking towards us, a massive gallery following closely behind.

'Afternoon,' I said as Lee Trevino passed me and lodged himself in the adjacent bay. Fate was having a ball. Within minutes four of the greatest wedge players in the world surrounded me. Watson, Crenshaw and Ballesteros had all joined Trevino, and by the look of it, so had half of Southport. I stood for a while not daring to hit, but after a much needed cigarette, I decided to give my right hand the ultimate test.

In the most masochistic way I decided to give my right hand one last chance; the ultimate showdown; a soft lob off a tight lie, in front of Seve, who was turned in my direction. At impact my whole body exploded and my soft lob, shot off along the ground like a ninety-yard putt. I looked up at Andy shaking my head.

'I'm sorry kid, but I can't play - not like this. I've got to withdraw.' His lack of reaction was the last nail in the coffin. It was the first time someone else acknowledged I was finished.

With the eyes of West Surrey on me, I couldn't withdraw with anything other than injury, and it had to be a pretty damn spectacular one. As I was contemplating a plan Andy came up with a great idea.

'Why not fall off the back of the buggy?' he suggested. I'd always liked Andy, it was one of the reasons I had invited him to caddie for me, but I'd never considered him to be particularly clever or inventive. It was time to reassess my assistant.

'That's a brilliant idea.' I said. It was like an episode from, Black Adder Goes Forth, when Rowan

Atkinson would try anything to avoid going 'over the top'. Well, there were no bullets left in my gun and wanting to avoid annihilation, we discussed exactly how to make the fall look realistic.

The buggy driver had driven far too fast when he had taken us to the practice ground. The plan involved falling off the buggy on the return journey, landing on my shoulder and screaming with pain as I hit the deck. It was a great plan – foolproof. I explained to Andy what I intended to do and then collected all my new gear from Titleist. I felt slightly guilty about doing that, but I could hardly say, 'I'd better not take it now; I'm just about to fall off a buggy.'

For over twenty minutes we waited for Sterling Moss to turn up. Finally he arrived in a cloud of dust skidding to a stop beside us. Andy got in the front, ready to shout 'Stop! I got on the back with all the new gear balanced strategically on my lap so when I fell off the disaster would look additionally spectacular.

True to form our driver set off at a fantastic pace throwing us from side to side and I was just about to let go of the side rail to take my dive, when incredibly the driver slowed to a crawl and glanced round. 'Think you've got much chance this week?' he asked.

Think I've got much chance!! I thought as Sterling Moss started to drive like an octogenarian. 'No,' I said forcefully, my terse monosyllabic answer hoping to prompt a return to speed.

'Got any tips then?'....

Five minutes later we got off the buggy in one piece; we could have walked faster. If I'd taken a dive at that speed I would have looked dodgier than Jurgen Klinsman in the penalty area.

'What now?' asked Andy.

'Going to tell them straight,' I said. 'No more messing about, I'm going to tell them that I've injured my shoulder and it's too painful to play.' With that deceptively brave statement, I stomped off to the Championship office to find the Royal and Ancient hierarchy.

'So I can't swing,' I said wincing while holding my injured shoulder. The director put his hand on my other shoulder in a gesture of sympathy. 'We've got a great physio here, I'll give him a call right now.'

Five minutes later we were down at the physio centre being looked at in the treatment room.

'I see,' said the physio. 'What terrible luck, but I think I can help. Cortisone, that's what you need. It might just do the trick.'

The nurse held my hand as the doc drove the needle deep into my perfectly good joint. At the time I remember thinking that I was not handling the situation very well!

After patching me up with a bandage, explaining the shoulder would be sore from the injection, we returned to our hotel with our new equipment. Andy had to carry it all as my shoulder was excruciating.

Very generously the R and A had suggested I wait until the day of the event before officially withdrawing, if I had to. That night TV, teletext, alerted all my supporters about my injury.

The hotel we'd booked into was so dilapidated we were the only golfers staying there and with nothing else to do, we kicked our heels for two days. There was no way I wanted to go back to the club and expose my swing to more practice, so I decided to wait out the time in Southport. I phoned the shop several times to see the reaction to my possible withdrawal, but everyone was convinced I would be fine. The only people who knew the whole story were Vanessa and my parents. Understandably they couldn't fully grasp the situation. No-one could.

'You can't let them down John, you can't, you've never seen anything like it. Everybody's travelling north to watch you!'

This was not good to hear - not good at all! I was in a no win situation. I'd hidden the complete breakdown of my game from everyone, but now, one way or the other, I would be exposed.

I didn't get much sleep on Tuesday and when I went to bed on Wednesday, having to sleep on my left side to avoid the pain made by the injection, I was virtually suicidal. I had gone to bed at eleven but had woken up at two. Three hours of tossing and turning hadn't been enough to refresh me, but something had happened during that time. As I slowly woke up, scared to move in case I lost the thread of my thoughts, I slowly reigned in the idea that had presented itself to me during my fretful sleep. After fifteen minutes I leapt out of bed, hit the light and stood naked in front of the mirror.

'What's going on?' asked Andy.

'Belt up kid; I think I've found something.'

Whether the pressure had acted as a catalyst or it was just 'the right time' but as I stood looking in the mirror, the secret to my swing was revealed. From somewhere deep down, the answer to all my questions burst forth and I saw the swing in absolute clarity. That clarity immediately pointed out where I had been going wrong for so many years and led me to the startling conclusion of what I had to do. Suddenly, I realised why my swing was steep and why I was so prone to 'yipping'. After all those years I had suddenly found the secret to my swing.

'You all right John? Andy asked obviously concerned. I'd been up for well over an hour trying to break down my theory, but what I had discovered was the piece of the jigsaw I had searched so hard to find. All those years ago, in my very first lesson, John Jacobs had diagnosed my problem accurately. I just hadn't been able to understand how altering my head position could alter my attack into the ball – until that morning. For a fleeting moment I thought about the thousands of wasted hours I had spent trying to find an answer to my swing, when the answer was there all the time. I turned to Andy as sunlight started to creep into the room.

'Go back to sleep kid, we're playing later.'

Chapter 14
Biting the Bullet

The morning of the first round of the Open Championship, I went for a long walk by the sea to calm my adrenaline sodden body. It was freezing. At eleven o'clock, the television beamed the first live broadcast from the course and I sat watching from the safety of the hotel room. My teeing off time was 3.42pm; we had a long time to wait.

Conditions at the club looked a complete nightmare with players wearing bobble hats and waterproofs to protect themselves from the strong wind. Apart from my awful form on links courses I always struggled in the cold and I had second thoughts about playing.

If I did make it to the first tee at least I would look the part. I was dressed in my new Titleist clothes, the designer of which must have had 'conspicuous' as a directive and although choosing the most somber sweater, I still felt like a detonating lightning bolt; red, black, white and yellow zigzagged across my chest. If all went wrong, I imagined I'd find a Titlist rep at the back of the 18th green holding up a blanket to cover me with a sign saying, 'He's not really one of ours'.

Every so often that morning I disappeared outside to have a swing. Many times in the past, during sleepless nights, I thought I had discovered a new theory only to have it disintegrate at dawn, but the new action felt secure, the reasoning behind it unshakable. Never the less, what I was about to try was crazy; a new stance on my least favorite course on planet earth...whilst suffering from the 'yips'. I cringed at the uncertainty and just hoped that my new swing would pacify my right hand twitch.

At two o'clock, the latest we could leave our journey to the course, Andy loaded up the car and we set off. I had hoped the atrocious weather to deter some of the spectators, but when we arrived at the course it was packed. It was even a struggle to walk from the car park to the clubhouse. At one point, the traffic jam left me near the entrance to the press tent, where out of morbid fascination I showed my players badge and popped in. So far it had been a quiet day, Faldo and Save around par and the news hounds looked hungry for that juicy morsel. 'God not me' I pleaded inwardly 'Please not me'.

Outside, all I could see happy smiling faces. What made that particularly bad news was they all seemed to be the happy smiling faces of people I knew; Lancashire had seemingly been invaded by members from West Surrey. I sought refuge on the putting green, but near the gate I spotted a large group of fanatics waving to me. The West Surrey gang was obviously keen to watch me warm up on the practice ground, but I had decided against putting my new action through unnecessary stress. I was relying totally on logic.

With my head turned to the right, something I had not tried properly since my lesson with John Jacobs, it would enable me to swing back on a more inside path. It hadn't worked before, because I didn't understand how the rest of my action would change. Hopefully, my attack on the ball would be shallower, which would mean I could hit the ball with my body releasing rather than last minute hand action at impact. I was now convinced my yipping had started after years of attacking the ball from a steep angle and I trusted that theory. Even so there was no way I was going to take any chances on the practice ground.

I waved back at my supporters, managed a weak smile and pulled my visor down so all I could see were people's feet.

As the minutes ticked by, my body overdosed on nerves and started to protest. I felt fragile, my stomach was knotted tight and with an hour to go before teeing off, I went into the locker room of the Royal Bridal Golf Club, locked myself in the toilet and threw up.

Above my head was an open window and outside I could hear the excitement of thousands of spectators lapping up the atmosphere. Inside, my heart was pounding and sweat poured off me. Had a vet seen me, he would have put me out of my misery. Kneeling in prayer I waited for the minutes to pass. In the locker room I had watched Jack Nicklaus getting ready to go out to play and he looked incredibly composed. I wondered if he had ever felt as bad as I did at that moment.

I have never known time to drag quite as interminably as those last few minutes, but at last destiny beckoned and it was time to make my way to the tee. Roger Davis the Australian had just hit off when I arrived at the starter's tent and neither of my playing partners, Martin Poxon nor Frederick Lindren had materialised. I took my driver and climbed the steps to the deserted gallows. Hundreds of pairs of eyes watched as 'Flash' dipped a toe in the atmosphere. It was even more intimidating than I remembered from my practice round. The long tee stretched away like an aircraft carrier runway. It looked impossibly narrow, hemmed in by the packed stands.

I thought about a practice swing using my new stance, but I decided to see what my normal swing felt like. Even on my practice swing my right hand detonated. It's tough to take a divot with a driver, but next time you play Birkdale, check out the back of the tee, two yards in from the plate. That old scar running forty-five degrees right is mine. It was a timely reminder to commit to my new theory. I walked off the tee to wipe my club to find Andy wiping his eye;

'Something in it?' I asked.

'Yeah, your divot,' he said. I realised then why Ivor, the starter, was wiping down his trousers. Finally the moment arrived.

'And on the tee, match number thirty eight, from England - John Hoskison.'

Twice my trembling hand knocked the ball off the tee peg and I hoped the thousands couldn't see my flapping trouser legs. I addressed the ball, tilted my head to the right, said a final prayer and swung back. For two days I had imagined what might happen to my first tee shot. I thought I'd covered every possible scenario, but there was one I hadn't considered. As the club came into impact, my right hand was in the perfect position and the ball took off like a bullet, dead straight, undeviating in flight. I had nailed a perfect shot right down the middle. Amidst the applause I made my way back to Andy and gripped the top of the bag to help keep me upright.

'Jesus what a shot,' said Andy. After the others hit he hoisted the impossibly heavy bag onto his back as if it was as light as a feather.

My second shot was from a similar position to where I had fatted my three iron forty yards in practice, but this time my swing felt silky smooth and the ball ripped to the heart of the green. When I looked at the ground, instead of my divot mark pointing left, it was dead straight. Unfortunately, whilst my right arm was quite content to remain passive when I hit full shots, on the greens it was just as twitchy and I only just managed to two putt, but incredibly I had made a par - a bloody par.

Another nailed drive at the second found me the longest off the tee but against the wind the hole was playing really long that day and I still needed a one iron to the green. Even at the best of times that's a tough club to use, but I will remember the quality of my next shot forever.

For the first time I understood that a pure strike feels as though the clubface collects the ball, compresses it to its absolute maximum, and then slings it forward like a stone from a slingshot. There's this delicious feeling of having the ball embedded in the blade, then releasing off with maximum control. To a golfer, that extra millisecond of contact is the Holy Grail. It's the feeling I had searched for throughout my career and as distinctive as the acceleration between a Ford Fiesta and Ferrari.

From two hundred yards, my one iron slung the ball forward with the accuracy of David when he nailed Goliath. It was an absolute ripper, climbing like Concorde, finally falling to the green to stop some ten feet short of the pin. The ensuing putt fell into the back of the cup to complete a perfectly played hole for birdie.

I couldn't believe it - I really couldn't believe

it. The roar from the gallery, albeit mainly members from West Surrey, was deafening and for the first time I pushed back my visor to take in the scene. My members stood on the hills looking down, a picture so vivid I can recall it at will. It was made even better when I arrived on the third tee to see the giant leader board showing me at one under par, lying in second place behind Nick Faldo and Seve Ballesteros.

But even with good shots on the first few holes, there was no sudden transformation of confidence, the scars left by past performances were far too deep to be wiped out so easily and every shot I hit that day was an individual battle.

It was nearly nine o'clock in the evening when we came to the final hole and in the gloom I had to aim my second shot at the clubhouse lights, as I couldn't see the flag. I didn't see my ball land and only realised it had found the green by the ripple of applause from the few brave spectators that had remained. The relief was enormous. Even at that stage I was only too aware of the out of bounds fences, the pot bunkers and the ever-present fear of having to pitch over one. But somehow, right to the end, I had continued to strike the ball with authority, my new swing keeping the scales tipped in favour of survival.

Despite several three putts and a dreadful piece of clubbing at the eleventh, I holed my last putt for a seventy-four. I had played in the toughest conditions, on a day that saw few scores below par and my result was beyond my wildest dreams. I walked off the course battle weary and shattered with fatigue. My eyes were sore through lack of sleep, and I felt as wobbly as a new-born colt. When we returned to the guesthouse I fell into bed exhausted.

****

When I was a little boy I used to have a recurring dream of a heavy pillow spinning on a small pin held lightly between my thumb and forefinger. For the first time in twenty years I had the dream that night. Andy said I only screamed out twice, but I must have been pretty active because in the morning I found my completely disheveled bedclothes on the floor. There had been little peace that night and it seemed only the blink of an eye before we were back in action.

When I stepped onto the tee to start my second round, on the scale of nerves from one to ten, I was still way up there, around nine-point-eight. Even after several holes of good striking, I still couldn't fully trust my action, but after completing the front nine holes in one over par, the first thoughts of trying to make the cut, broke through my survival mode to confuse me.

I had achieved everything I could possibly have hoped for; a performance good enough for me to return to West Surrey with my head held high. But my instincts were pressing me to make the cut and masochistically take another two days of risk and torture.

It was a juggling act of incredible skill to keep both options open and when I came to the thirty sixth hole I needed a par four to qualify for the last two rounds. Intellectually I knew I should quit. Instinctively I was still trying and the confusion made me hit my only inaccurate drive of the two rounds. The ball sliced away to the right and buried itself in a bush. Immediately, I felt deflated. As I walked off the tee the anti-climax was monumental and I found it ironic that it was only when I had blown my chance, did I realise how much I had wanted the dream to continue. Having remained pretty quiet for two days, it was Andy who managed to find the right words to pump me up.

'You've got to keep trying Hoski - all the members have bet on you to make the cut.'

'They've what?!'

'Yeah, big money. You know what they're like. They put the money on this morning - told me not to tell you.'

I looked left to where I could see all my supporters walking down the eighteenth and I decided to have one last monumental effort.

After declaring my ball unplayable I had to take a penalty drop. The only place I could find not totally swamped by thick rough but still keeping the bush between me and the flag, was near a mole hill some two hundred and sixty yards from the green. It was a bit of a gamble trying to land it on such a specific place, but when I dropped the ball it remained on a slight upslope like a launch pad. After checking with the rules official that everything had been carried out correctly, I contemplated the shot. The ball was lying pretty well and the shot was downwind, but two hundred and sixty yards. I looked across at the West Surrey gang, hoping I could do something to impress them. As if drawing Excalibur from its scabbard, I then pulled out my one iron.

It is probably the most powerful shot I have ever hit. Every sinew, every muscle fiber went into creating speed. I swung at the ball as hard as I could, throwing in some violence for good measure. The impact on the moles home must have been like a '747' tearing off its roof, but the strike was perfect and the ball took off like a missile. I knew it was good but I couldn't see it clearly because the bush was in the way, so I looked across at the gang for feedback.

At first there was silence, then applause,

building to a roaring crescendo as my ball, unbeknown to me, ran onto the green and came to a stop some twenty feet from the pin. It was the most spectacular shot I had ever hit; only made more unbelievable when my putt dropped for me to make the cut on 147, eventually with a shot to spare. It was the most amazing mix of emotions. Exhilaration that I had achieved the impossible, but confusion I had chosen to take two further days of the unknown.

****

Two days later, on Sunday afternoon, last day of the Championship, I stood in the middle of the eighteenth fairway waiting to play my final shot to a green surrounded by packed stands. I had shot 74 in the third round, not with quite the same precision because the effort of demolishing the molehill had made my shoulder extremely tender. It was hard to believe it was the same week as having cortisone injected into it.

Eventually the players in front vacated the last green, and it was time to confront the final hurdle. Even at that late stage danger lurked and any sort of a miscue might leave me with a delicate lob over a trap in front of fourteen thousand spectators. No thanks!

My final swing, with a five iron, felt the same as many that week. Without a practice shot during the event, the new swing had stood up to unimaginable pressure, proving beyond doubt I had found the secret. The ball slung away directly at the pin coming to rest in the middle of the green and finally, I was able to relax, step away from the abyss and absorb the heady atmosphere of playing the last hole in a major.

I have a film of those last few minutes given to

me by a member who had smuggled in a video camera beneath his coat. Whenever I watch it, it brings a tear to my eye. I see a man occasionally waving to the crowd, showing appreciation for the applause, smiling, appearing calm, but I know how that man felt inside and it is so different to how he looks.

That unique walk of two hundred yards brought my journey to an end. A journey that had lasted over a week and had taken me down a rare path. In a week I had travelled the complete emotional spectrum from absolute despair, to unsurpassed exhilaration.

Throughout the week my twitch on the greens had cost me valuable shots but I two putted the final green to score a closing round of 71. Not only had I survived the final hurdle, but I had produced my lowest score of the tournament.

Just before driving home we were in the car park when the chairman of West Surrey came to shake my hand.

'John - you're a star,' he said.

I smiled. I had felt like one all day. The Titleist Tour clothes designer, proving himself a colour-blind schizophrenic, had far outstripped his previous three design attempts taking 'conspicuous' to new heights. The pattern on my sweater that day was literally stunning. I knew it was power dressing by the reaction of the players in front of me when I had earlier stepped onto the first tee and whipped off my waterproof jacket. Both Craig Stadler and Tom Weiskopf looked stunned.

'Wow,' said Craig. 'You should warn people before you do that.'

Chapter 15
You Know I Never Hit Balls

My old boss Jack Busson used to equate golfers with cars but I saw them more as thoroughbred racehorses. Nick Faldo would be the ultimate Derby runner; trained and primed purely for the classic, his jockey would only have to kick him out of the stalls, point him in the right direction and enjoy the ride.

Seve, definitely a Grand National runner, would require a little more horsemanship. Apart from the odd bite you might get, show him Beeches Brook and he would be flat out at take off. The ultimate crowd pleaser, who'd literally leave you breathless.

You'd have to run Greg Norman in blinkers and hide him in the pack until the last moment, then ignite the rocket in the last furlong. The acceleration would likely tear your arms from sockets, but if you could hang on, you'd win. Myself? Well, the trainer would need to be a very clever man, the jockey a bloody genius.

Confidence is a strange thing. I once thought if you had it, you had it in everything, but I found out that is not the case. It can be extremely specific and whilst many thought my performance in the Open was due to a new 'inner peace' they were wrong. I had confidence, but only when it came to a full swing;

ask me to pitch over a trap or hole a tricky downhill putt and I would transform from a confident looking animal into a twitchy, rolling eyed colt.

My new swing however, elevated me to a new class and when I returned from the Open my striking enabled me to capture the three remaining PGA events of the year. My most pleasing came in the PGA Southern Championships, open to over seven hundred pros and played round the monstrous East Sussex National. The previous two years I hadn't even made the cut and normally the sheer length of the course defeated me, but with an extra twenty five yards off the tee and new found ability to strike long irons, I shot 66 - 69, nine under for the last thirty six holes, to come through to win my first major title. I had never won anything of note. To blitz such a strong field was an amazing feeling.

From July, right through to the end of the season I was caught up with 'playing fever' and when the winter months came I was pleased to take a rest. Even though West Surrey had instigated my return to playing, I felt guilty at being absent from the club and I often tried to cover up that I was in action. I was also a little embarrassed by my success. Not to look as though I was bragging, I used to hide my trophies under the workbench in the shop. One day Ralph the secretary came in just as Andy was stashing away another.

'What are all those cups?' he asked pointing to the array of silverware.

'Oh' I said taken aback. 'Just bits and bobs.'

Ralph had none of it. 'Just bits and bobs?!' he said aghast.

Fifteen minutes later the West Surrey trophy cabinet was brimming over with my recently acquired

Championship trophies. In the last half of the year I had won the four most important events I could play in with a stroke average of 68.25.

When the 1992 season arrived, I knew I had a busy schedule ahead so decided to organize a golf day for the members to say 'thank you' for their expected support. Nearly the whole club turned out for my first 'Pros Day' and over a seven-hour stint I started them all off the first hole. The event was a great success, and when I headed for the National Club Professional Championships in July, I was able to leave the club with confidence.

The National Championship at St Pierre Country Club was my playing goal for the year. I had finished last in my two previous attempts at Sandwich and Carnoustie, so when I turned up, I wasn't exactly favourite. I also employed a game plan that led many to believe I was not taking the event seriously; no practice shots, no practice round and I arrived late the day before the first round to register and find a caddie.

Renton Doig was the professional at St Pierre and late in the afternoon I walked into his shop to see if there was anyone left to carry my bag in the tournament. I was told all the regular caddies and junior members had been booked, except one young boy named Jason. I found him sitting outside with his older friends, looking much younger than his fourteen years and small enough to fit inside my tour bag. After seeing his small frame, I doubted whether he could do the job, but when I asked if he wanted to caddie, his face lit up with enthusiasm.

Even with his obvious will, I still doubted he could manage and as a trial, we wandered out to my car and unloaded my golf bag, which I placed on his back. It dwarfed him.

'You'd better use a trolley tomorrow,' I suggested. Immediately his face blanched.

'No, no, let me carry it, I can do it honestly - my brother's carrying.' I looked at him and smiled. I knew what it was like to be the smallest and against my better judgment, I agreed.

'Don't let me down Jason,' I warned.

The next day I struck the ball beautifully. I nailed every shot and although I missed several short putts, I shot 67, five under par, to be joint leader. In the second and third rounds my solid striking continued and incredibly, with only one round to go, I had pulled six shots clear of the field. I had never led by such a large margin and all I could think of was the similar lead Gil Morgan had blown earlier that year in the US Open.

Jason, my young caddie had been excellent throughout the three days, never once floundering under the weight of the bag, keeping up with my fast walk and oozing a contagious enthusiasm at every turn, but when I met him before the last round he looked less exuberant than normal. The previous day he'd been really looking forward to the final round, especially the prospect of appearing on Sky TV, who were covering the final stages, but his normally smiling face was clouded with worry. With only half an hour to go, before being announced on the tee, I turned to him; 'What's the problem Jason?'

'Nothing.'

'Yes there is. I don't want to worry about you - now tell me.' He hesitated before confessing. 'My brother said you don't hit balls on the practice ground because you don't trust me to pick them up.'

I looked down at him. 'That's rubbish,' I said. 'I

told you. I never hit balls.' It was especially true that week as the pros had to hit their own.

'I told him that, but he didn't believe me' Jason said as tears welled up in his eyes. 'I told my mum I'd be picking them up today, and now she's turned up to watch with my brother.'

He pointed to a car some fifty yards away where I could see two people sitting inside taking shelter from the drizzle. His brother wasn't in action as the pro he'd been caddying for had missed the cut.

'Jason, you idiot,' I sighed. It was the sort of stupid situation I'd got myself into many times before and even though slightly annoyed, I empathised with him. I glanced across at the practice ground, which was deserted as nearly all the other players were already on the course.

'Look, there's no way I'm hitting balls before I play, but I'll pretend to hit a few with some practice swings. No one will be able to tell the difference if we go to the far side, they're too far away. If it's that important to you, go to the top of the range and after I've had a swing, bend down and pick up an imaginary ball. No one will know, it's too drizzly to see. Want to do that?'

His face lit up. 'Yeah' he said.

For the next fifteen minutes I stood on the deserted practice ground hitting imaginary balls to my distant caddie. I would fire a drive, then seconds later Jason would bend down to pick it up. He was a bit unimaginative with his movement and stood in one spot for much of the time, but on the whole it was pretty authentic. The drizzle was just enough to keep mum and brother in the car and from more than a hundred yards there was no way anyone could have guessed.

'Don't tell your mum stories in future,' I said to him sternly after calling him back. As we passed his car on our way to the first tee his mum and brother gave us a little wave. His brother was smiling and looking suitably impressed.

Shortly after we teed off, the drizzle turned to rain, but even in the lousy weather Jason, using towels, sweater, shirt and eventually the top of his underpants, managed to keep the clubs dry. He proved equal to any caddie I had employed, but it was a tough day to score on. By the time we had reached the ninth hole, I was one over par for the day, my lead down to a single shot.

Surprisingly the dreadful weather had not deterred the locals from turning up and there was quite a good atmosphere. There was one particular spectator I was delighted to see. Roger Davidson a member of West Surrey, and a director at Shell, had been travelling to London when he'd seen an article about the tournament in the Daily Telegraph. At Clapham he had changed trains, returned home, grabbed his gear and caught the first available train to Wales to watch me on the closing holes.

When I was just having a moment of doubt that I could convert my lead, his presence was enough to spur me on for that extra effort and over the back nine I played superb golf to re-establish my six shot lead. On the last hole, I fired a two iron to the front edge of the famous eighteenth and in front of Sky cameras, colleagues and hardy spectators; I finished off to win the National PGA Professional Championships. As I raised my arms aloft and accepted the applause, I thought back to my experience at Carnoustie when I had thought it all over. Re-born through technique, I was a very lucky man.

Prize giving, presentations and press interviews followed where most questions were aimed at the forthcoming PGA Cup match against the Americans. On a more personal nature, PGA officials pointed out that winning the Championship meant I held every major PGA title I was eligible to hold. The following day they called it the Club Pros Grand Slam, never having been achieved before, unlikely, they said, to happen again. Considering I had finished rock bottom in every event the previous year it was some come back. I had won The National Club Pros, The Southern Pros Championships, the Southern CP Championships, the Surrey Open, and the Surrey PGA all in a matter of a few months. After the press had asked their questions I was allowed to go and I wandered out carrying the splendid trophy to find Jason sheltering in the car with his mum and brother. I had already agreed with mum that she would cash a cheque for him and I handed over our agreed fee. Twenty pounds a round plus five percent of my winnings. An extravagant contract for a novice caddie, but he had proved to be an absolute gem. I lent in, shook his hand and gave him a cheque for three hundred and eighty pounds. He beamed back.

'Couldn't have done it without you Jason – thanks. Let me know what you spend it on.'

A month later I received a letter telling me that he'd become the proud owner of his first set of clubs; Mizuno TP9's - same set as myself.

After Jason left I was finally about to leave when a car pulled up beside mine and one of the competitors, who had finished in the top ten, wound down his window.

'Well done John, we knew you'd win today. A couple of us were waiting on the first tee and saw you hitting shots on the practice ground. Best session I've seen. Your caddie hardly moved a yard all the time we watched. Certainly got that swing taped.'

When I eventually left the club and made my way home, I couldn't help smile as I thought about my 'legendary' practice session.

Chapter 16
Success at Last

In the months following my victory at Chepstow I managed to retain all the trophies I had won the previous season. It meant I had won the last eight important events I had played in and throughout I had struck the ball in a way I had never thought possible. During that time I never hit a practice shot. I just rehearsed my technique using practice swings in my back garden and perfecting my stance in the mirror.

My victories also brought several fantastic spinoffs. Not only was I the lead player in the PGA Cup matches against the USA at the K Club in Ireland but I was also invited to play in the USA Club Professionals Championships in America. Open to all 27,000 PGA pros in the States, the standard is always very high and no European Player had ever made the cut. But with my swing operating as consistently as ever I managed to finish 15th and pick up another healthy cheque as well as a bonus cheque from Titleist, just for using their ball. It was an amazing time for me. Instead of constantly worrying about my swing, when I teed up my ball I knew I would be able to negotiate even the toughest holes in the worst weather. Finally I could control the flight of my ball in a left to right wind.

My success on the course had led to several articles appearing in local and national papers about my transformation from hacker to champion, and on the suggestion of the sports editor of the Surrey Advertiser, I set about writing down my thoughts about the swing in a series of instructional articles

The articles were very well received and shortly after they appeared, I was asked by Nick Wright, the instruction editor of Golf Monthly, to put together some articles for his national magazine.

After the articles appeared, more and more people starting phoning up for lessons and I found myself spending most of my time teaching golf and writing about it. Unintentionally I was taking a step back from playing golf, concentrating instead on teaching it. It seemed my inexhaustible efforts to find the secret of my own swing had inadvertently given me the knowledge to sort out other peoples' problems.

Golf Monthly were obviously pleased with the reaction from their readers. One day Nick Wright invited me to the headquarters of Golf Monthly in London and outlined a project that involved putting my swing theories on film. They wanted me to go to Valderamma in Spain and make a video using my 'fascinating analogies,' which they would give out free with every magazine.

It was a fantastic opportunity. The project would take my reputation as a teacher to new heights and I relished the prospect. I was getting great satisfaction watching my pupils improve, and the thought of being able to air my views to thousands was a tremendous prospect. I set about writing down my thoughts in a script and waited for a date to be set in the diary when filming could take place in the sun.

The members at West Surrey were thrilled to

see their club professional succeed in this new way, but their respect for me went into orbit two days before the 1993 Ryder Cup. Due to the special relationship I had forged with the USPGA hierarchy during my appearances in the PGA Cup matches and my visit to America, the President, Captain and Secretary of the USPGA turned up to West Surrey to have lunch with me. They turned up in limousines wearing their official Ryder Cup blazers looking absolutely stunning and it blew the minds of my members.

Ralph the Captain and committee joined us in the restaurant and it was an absolutely fabulous day. Knowing how tight their schedule was and that there visit to see me was the only stop off before the opening ceremony of the Ryder Cup, as a compliment it was about as good as it gets.

After the summer ended a date was chosen for our trip to Spain and I couldn't wait to start filming. But the week before we were due to fly out a problem cropped up with the film technicians and the trip was postponed to a later date. It was very disappointing but having seen the professionalism of the production team when they had taken special pictures for my articles; I knew that everything had to be right.

Although disappointed, at least the delay gave me an opportunity to organize the next round of a match play competition that I had entered with a friend of mine. It was a match play event and we were due to play the next round against the professional and his amateur partner from the Drift Country Club. With my trip abroad postponed, it seemed an ideal opportunity to get the match played.

In mid November, three days before the match I was struck down by a tummy bug. For three days I lay in bed hardly able to open my eyes and it felt as though someone had kicked me round the course.

In normal circumstances I would have withdrawn from the match; I felt very weak in the morning not having eaten for three days, but I decided against cancelling as we were already overdue with the result.

I was definitely not myself. For the first time in twenty years I turned up to compete to find I had forgotten my putter. I hadn't bothered to check my equipment, I'd been too tired, and I had to borrow a putter from the pro at the Drift. Fortunately it was a nice day, overcast but warm, and we had a pretty enjoyable game, the fresh air a welcome relief after being stuck in a stuffy room for three days, but I was shattered when we finished.

For twenty years I had travelled to golf events and had maintained a discipline of not drinking and driving. It was a routine I had got into, especially when on foreign territory. But that day, inexplicably, I accepted a glass of wine. My friends didn't realize I hadn't eaten anything for three days and that I had nothing inside me to line my stomach. I asked at the bar for a sandwich, anything to eat, but it was late and the kitchen was closed. The wine went straight through me.

Somewhere in the back of my mind I knew I was heading down a dangerous path but I just couldn't quite process the warning. Then, caught up in a conversation about my proposed trip, catastrophically I accepted another glass when it was offered.

Half an hour later I left the club and on my short journey home .....I hit and killed a cyclist.

The Final Chapter

I'm writing this last chapter twenty years after finishing the manuscript you have just read. I'm so sorry to have surprised you in such an awful way, and I wish I could just be talking about my exciting time as a successful teacher and my video in Spain. But it didn't turn out that way. Taking the risk just once caused complete devastation.

The day after the accident I offered my resignation to West Surrey and the PGA, but far harder I had to sit my parents down and my family and explain I would be going to prison. The only thing that kept me going through those dark days was the forgiveness I received from the widow who went as far as to ask for leniency to be shown to me at my sentencing trial. It was the most generous gift any man could receive.

In November 1994, at the Old Bailey law courts in London, Lord Justice Hooper sentenced me to three years, and when he banged his gavel, I picked up my Mizuno overnight bag and embarked on a journey that I would not wish on anyone.

The only thing I knew about prison was what my paper told me. During my time at West Surrey some criminals had stolen a large van and had come crashing through the front wall of my shop. They demolished the building and stole all my stock. While the shop was being rebuilt I had to live in it for security purposes. Just about that time, an article appeared in my paper telling me what would happen to the criminals if they were caught. They would be banged up in a 'holiday camp', with marvelous educational facilities, great gyms and cordon bleu food served in the canteens. It used to make my blood boil that we could treat criminals in such a lenient way. Little did I know that one day I was to experience prison myself.

I'm sure everyone reading this book was expecting a story about golf, so I will not go into what happened to me in prison at this time. Suffice to say, I was so shocked at the conditions and treatment of some of the young men, I wrote a book called Inside – One Man's Experience of Prison. Lord Ramsbotham, Her Majesty's Chief Inspector of Prisons, said it was a very 'brave and important book' and it did take some courage to have it published. But I'm glad I did – several things have been improved in the prison system because of it.

Looking back at those terrible days, it was probably only my age and experience that saved me from getting hooked on drugs or beaten to pulp. Prison was like my old boarding school... but on steroids. I owe a lot to Mike Hart and the guys on 'A wing' who kept me safe.

The day I was released as a free man, I literally sank to my knees in thanks. It had been a difficult time, spending my sentence in some of the toughest prisons in the country, with some very dangerous men, but somehow I had survived. Prison's not meant to be easy, in fact the harder the regime the better as far as I'm concerned. But prison should be fair and offer some sort of hope to the young men who want to go straight. It doesn't quite work out like that. After my release it was difficult to see I had any future at all.

The catalyst for my attempt to claw my way back to something like my former life came from the incredible forgiveness shown to me; not only from the widow but also from my former colleagues. As far as they were concerned I had paid my debt and they just wanted to see me back. But golf was the last thing on my mind.

I had witnessed terrible violence in prison and I wanted to balance the views traditionally held by the media. For several years I embarked on a project trying to warn youngsters about the dangers of taking unnecessary risks and I travelled the length and breadth of England speaking at schools. It was helpful for them and it was cathartic for me. Then, out of the blue, in 2005 I was asked to enter a golf tournament. It was a real shock to my system.

Tony Jones the organizer of the newly formed Jamega Tour phoned me up to see if I would like to play. Initially I blanched at the thought, but encouraged by friends and family, I eventually decided to enter.

It's pretty hard to describe how nervous I was the first day of the event; I'd hardly hit a shot for ten years. In the buildup I had ventured to a local driving range to see if I could remember how to hit a ball and had been surprised how quickly my body recaptured the feel of my swing. But it was hardly good preparation and my clubs had definitely seen better days. I hadn't seen them for almost ten years. My mother and father had looked after them with my other personal possessions. In my bag was my old Taylor Made driver, which had a slight crack in the face and my irons had not been cleaned since my last round at West Surrey.

When the starter announced me on the first tee I felt decidedly sick. I remember seeing my trouser leg flapping as my knees shook, but somehow I made a smooth swing. When I looked after my ball, I couldn't believe it was travelling like a rocket down the middle of the fairway.

In the first round at Frilford Heath I shot 67. In the final round I kept trusting my swing, relying on the technique that had proved so successful years before. With my accuracy off the tee lasting out, I went on to win the event by four shots. Over the next month I won five out of six tournaments. Incredibly my swing had stood the test of time and the theory that had been born from the pressure of playing in the Open Championship at Royal Birkdale had proved correct.

While the event at Frilford had been a significant point in my life, for the next few years I lived in a strange world where I mixed two different lifestyles. I still spoke at schools where I constantly relived my time in prison, yet I dabbled with golf when I had the time. However, in 2007 as I was coming up to 50, I had an opportunity to take my player's card for the European Seniors PGA Tour and I decided to enter.

When I ventured to Portugal it was incredible seeing and hearing about my old friends; Dave Williams had become a top tour rules official and Barry Lane had become a Ryder Cup star. It was like going back in a time warp.

After grinding out six rounds of classic tour school pressure I managed to finish 2nd and gain a card to play the following season. I wasn't quite sure how everyone would take that, but my parents and all my friends were thrilled. So was the hierarchy at the European Tour who wrote me an incredibly kind letter. For the next six months I waited impatiently for my return to tour golf. My first event was to be in Poland, the week after my 50th birthday.

Very nervously in 2008 I played in the Polish Senior Open near Krakow. Playing with Pete Oakley, the 2004 Senior Open Champion and Jean Pierre Sallat, I opened up birdie, par, eagle and went on to shoot 71. In the second round I played with Ryder Cup Captain Ian Woosnam. It was also his first event as a senior and when we shook hands on the first tee, I couldn't help but remember back to when I had first met him as a fourteen year old.

As far as striking was concerned, even at fifty, he seemed as good as ever and he went on to win in a desperately exciting finish before flying back to Jersey in his private jet. I played okay but scored terribly to finish a mediocre 40th, returning to Gatwick on a packed Easyjet flight.

It was a year later and over a decade after leaving prison I knew my life had travelled full circle. I had qualified for the Seniors Open Championship at Royal Troon and incredibly had made the cut. On the last day I stood on the practice ground with the likes of Tom Watson and Greg Norman, waiting to venture out for the fourth round. Tom and the boys were undoubtedly thinking about the first tee shot, I was contemplating life. It had been an incredible journey; from struggling as a young tour player to surviving in prison and then once again having an opportunity to compete. It was such a privilege to be standing on the practice ground, feeling the familiar surge of pre match nerves before playing against golfing legends. It has been an undeniable thrill playing golf as a professional.

As the 2013 season beckons hopefully the excitement is not all over yet. This coming year I have a few important projects to deal with first. I'm shortly travelling up to spend the day at a Secure Unit in the north of England where some of England's most troubled youngsters are housed. I've been there before and it's a tough day – the last speaker ran out after ten minutes.

Then, after a few more engagements at schools and young offender institutions, in August I might be playing again. Last year, because of a leg injury and commitments to schools, I entered only one tournament, the British Senior Professional Championships. I finished third. That good result is making me contemplate having a final fling round the course that pretty much sums up my golf and my life.

In two months time, the Senior Open Championship is taking place at Royal Birkdale. No kidding! I'm not sure whether that's fate knocking on my door, but it certainly feels like it. I can almost feel the course beckoning to me. I haven't studied the entry form yet, it was sent to me by the European Tour and it's sitting in a pile of papers on my desk. But every night, as distant memories come flooding back, I get a bit closer to having a look. Even if not this year, perhaps one day I will venture back...

****

To read how John Hoskison coped in prison (written in the same style as No Hiding in The Open) please read -
Inside - One Man's Experience of Prison.

If you're a golfer struggling to hit the ball well read the book, A Golf Swing You Can Trust. In it John describes the swing that transformed his game.

If you have any questions you would like to ask John, please email him at *hoskison51@hotmail.com*

Printed in Great Britain
by Amazon